THE Change YOU WANT TO SEE

A Culturally Responsive and Affirming Approach to
School
Leadership

**Dawn Brooks DeCosta
and Mark Anthony Gooden**

Solution Tree | Press

Copyright © 2025 by Solution Tree Press

Materials appearing here are copyrighted. With one exception, all rights are reserved. Readers may reproduce only those pages marked "Reproducible." Otherwise, no part of this book may be reproduced or transmitted in any form or by any means (electronic, photocopying, recording, or otherwise) without prior written permission of the publisher.

555 North Morton Street
Bloomington, IN 47404
800.733.6786 (toll free) / 812.336.7700
FAX: 812.336.7790

email: info@SolutionTree.com
SolutionTree.com
Visit go.SolutionTree.com/leadership to download the free reproducibles in this book.

Printed in the United States of America

Library of Congress Cataloging-in-Publication Data

Names: DeCosta, Dawn Brooks, author. | Gooden, Mark A., 1971- author.
Title: The change you want to see : a culturally responsive and affirming approach to school leadership / Dawn Brooks DeCosta, Mark Anthony Gooden.
Description: Bloomington, IN : Solution Tree Press, 2025. | Includes bibliographical references and index.
Identifiers: LCCN 2024040154 (print) | LCCN 2024040155 (ebook) | ISBN 9781954631410 (paperback) | ISBN 9781954631427 (ebook)
Subjects: LCSH: Educational leadership--Social aspects. | Educational change--Social aspects. | School management and organization--Social aspects. | Affective education. | Culturally relevant pedagogy.
Classification: LCC LB2806 .D39 2025 (print) | LCC LB2806 (ebook) | DDC 371.2/011--dc23/eng/20240917
LC record available at https://lccn.loc.gov/2024040154
LC ebook record available at https://lccn.loc.gov/2024040155

Solution Tree
Jeffrey C. Jones, CEO
Edmund M. Ackerman, President

Solution Tree Press
President and Publisher: Douglas M. Rife
Associate Publishers: Todd Brakke and Kendra Slayton
Editorial Director: Laurel Hecker
Art Director: Rian Anderson
Copy Chief: Jessi Finn
Production Editor: Madonna Evans
Copy Editor: Mark Hain
Cover and Text Designer: Julie Csizmadia
Acquisitions Editors: Carol Collins and Hilary Goff
Content Development Specialist: Amy Rubenstein
Associate Editors: Sarah Ludwig and Elijah Oates
Editorial Assistant: Anne Marie Watkins

Acknowledgments

Giving honor to my ancestors: I would like to offer my deepest gratitude for my parents, Anna Louise Blackwell Brooks and my late father, Robert Emanuel Brooks, my angels on earth and in heaven. My parents have consistently, since my birth, encouraged me to follow my gifts. They nurtured them, celebrated them, and provided opportunities for me to grow, learn, and share my gifts.

For my family: my husband, Roy M. DeCosta, my children, Kiani, Zoe, Phoenix, and Willow, and my grandchildren, Sage, Savannah, Soleil, Sincere, and Kaia, thank you for the love and support for all I do. You are my constant inspiration. Thank you for allowing me the time to do the work I love. To my extended family, the Blackwell and the Brooks families, thank you for your love and your prayers. I am eternally grateful to Brother Edward and St. Gabriel's School, Elizabeth Jarrett and the Harriet Tubman Learning Center, Dr. Sean L. Davenport and my Thurgood Marshall Academy Lower School (TMALS) family (staff, families, and students—I *love* you still and miss being with you daily). My TMALS art team (BJ, Tieee, Denise, Michelle, and Pam for being there for *every* idea I had), the late Dr. Calvin O. Butts III, Abyssinian Development Corporation, Dr. Sandye Johnson, and the Harlem Renaissance Education Pipeline (Ocynthia, Lori, Princess, and Kyla) for believing in me, celebrating, supporting, and trusting me.

To my beloved collaborators at Teachers College, Columbia University: Dr. Craig Richards, the Summer Principals Academy, Dr. Ellie Drago Severson, and my amazing coauthor, Dr. Mark A. Gooden, professor in the Urban Education Leaders Program, from whom I learned so much. For Dr. Sonya Douglass and the Black Education Research Center for the constant love and support for my work and the push to forge onward. To Harlem Community School District 5, I am so grateful for your collaboration and for the MECCA vision.

For the beloved partners I have had the joy to work with over the years and the leaders who believed in me and in TMALS: Dr. Marc Brackett, Dr. Robin Stern, Chi Kim, Dolores Esposito, Colin Lieu, Lisa Mazzola, Francis Estrada, Larissa Rafael, and Shanta Scott Lawson. For my mentor, artist, educator, activist, feminist, and storyteller, the late Faith Ringgold, for shaping my career through the beauty of the arts, and her daughters Michelle and Barbara, who I consider sisters. To my dearest and closest friends, Ife, Kamaria, and James, for allowing me to laugh, debrief, cry, and vent. Finally, I thank Harlem, NYC! I am in *love* with Harlem and have been for almost thirty years. To the people of the Harlem community, your beauty inspires me daily. Harlem is the mecca! I pray that all that manifests as a result of this book is in accordance with divine will, done under grace and in a perfect way, in harmony for the whole world. I thank the universe for the opportunity and strength to be a vessel in any way I have been and continue to be in the service of others.

—Dawn Brooks DeCosta

I am thankful to God, who constantly sends "angels" to my aid because I need them. As such, I am deeply appreciative of my wife, Angela Gooden, and daughter, Nia Ayanna Gooden, for their patience and kindness toward me as I have worked long hours to flow on several projects, including this one. I am thankful to my coauthor, Dr. Dawn Brooks DeCosta, for her leadership that came in the form of rich collaborative thinking, timely reminders, and just pure inspiration as we worked together on this "idea that became a book" project. Thanks to my graduate assistant Eve Murphy.

I am appreciative of a multitude of ancestors who continue to inspire me along the way and mentors (such as Linda C. Tillman) who encourage and support me as I seek to build a better world and pass along all that's been given to me and more. Thanks to my students, who have granted me the honor to teach and learn with them. I especially thank extended family, who have motivated me since my very early days of struggling to be emotionally OK, especially my *uplifting aunties* Zola Mims Davis, Velma Bobb, Louise Simmons, and Susan Lowery and *uplifting uncle* Curtis Simmons. I also appreciate my lovely cousins Debra Mims and Jeanelle Cornelius for their consistent support and guidance.

Thanks to Leslie P. Heard, who saw leadership early in my college days and lovingly and firmly nudged me to be more. Thanks to my two Alpha Phi Alpha Fraternity, Inc. brothers Ken Dyer and H. Rich Milner, who both have encouraged me immensely over the years. Thanks to my academic high school teacher-mother Mrs. Judy Thomas, who motivated me to lead, embrace the elegance and beauty of mathematics, and see things I could not yet see in myself. I also appreciate the late William Webb, who provided a solid example of an African American man teaching mathematics, coaching sports, and leading with heart.

Last but not least, I stand in deep appreciation of my late mother, Ida Mae Gooden, who remains my first and most beloved teacher. I miss you, I love you, and I remain inspired by what you envisioned for me so long ago.

—Mark Anthony Gooden

Solution Tree Press would like to thank the following reviewers:

Chris Bennett
Principal
Burns Middle School
Lawndale, North Carolina

Becca Bouchard
Educator
Calgary, Alberta, Canada

Tricia Brickner
Principal
Jefferson Elementary School
Goshen, Indiana

Molly Capps
Principal
McDeeds Creek Elementary School
Southern Pines, North Carolina

Jenna Fanshier
Principal
Marion Elementary School
Marion, Kansas

Melissa Saenz
Principal
Montwood Middle School
El Paso, Texas

Sherry Shin
Principal
Mason Crest Elementary
Annandale, Virginia

Steven Weber
Associate Superintendent for Teaching and Learning
Fayetteville Public Schools
Fayetteville, Arkansas

Visit **go.SolutionTree.com/leadership** to download the free reproducibles in this book.

Table of Contents

Reproducibles are in italics

About the Authors	xi
Introduction	1
Words From a Principal	4
About This Book	5
Questions for Reflection and Discussion	6
Chapter 1: Understanding Social-Emotional Learning and Culturally Responsive School Leadership	9
Words From a Principal	9
Words From a Professor	10
Social-Emotional Learning	11
Words From a Principal	14
SEL Benefits and Limitations	15
Culturally Responsive School Leadership	19
Transformational Leaders	20
An SEL Approach Centered in Cultural Responsiveness	22
Words From a Principal	26
Conclusion	26
Questions for Reflection and Discussion	27
Potential Action Steps	28

Chapter 2: Practicing Culturally Responsive and Affirming Social-Emotional Leadership (CRASEL) — 31

    Words From a Principal — 32
    Words From a Professor — 33
    Definitions of Key Terms — 34
    A Culture of Care — 36
    Words From a Principal — 41
    CRASEL Origins — 41
    The CRASEL Framework — 45
    Conclusion — 48
    Questions for Reflection and Discussion — 49
    Potential Action Steps — 50

Chapter 3: Prioritizing Self-Care — 53

    Words From a Principal — 53
    Words From a Professor — 55
    Self-Care, Self-Awareness, and Self-Management — 57
    The Importance of Self-Care — 58
    How to Establish a Self-Care Practice — 60
    Words From a Principal — 61
    Conclusion — 63
    Questions for Reflection and Discussion — 63
    Self-Care Reflection — 64
    Potential Action Steps — 65

Chapter 4: Engaging in Racial Reflection — 67

    Words From a Principal — 68
    Words From a Professor — 69
    The Racial Autobiography: A Culturally Responsive Leadership Practice — 71
    The Importance of Racial Reflection — 74
    A Schoolwide Vision for Racial Equity — 76
    Words From a Principal — 78
    Conclusion — 79
    Questions for Reflection and Discussion — 79
    Racial Autobiography Reflection — 80
    Potential Action Steps — 81

Chapter 5: Building School and Community Relationships **83**
- Words From a Principal 83
- Words From a Professor 85
- The Importance of Relational Trust 86
- How to Strengthen Community Relationships 87
- Words From a Principal 91
- Co-Creation and Co-Liberation 93
- Conclusion 97
- Questions for Reflection and Discussion 97
- *Community Relationship-Building Reflection* 98
- *Potential Action Steps* 99

Chapter 6: Committing to Advocacy **101**
- Words From a Principal 102
- Words From a Professor 103
- Advocacy and Social Justice Leadership 104
- The Advocate Leader 105
- Words From a Principal 109
- Conclusion 111
- Questions for Reflection and Discussion 111
- *Advocacy Leadership Reflection* 112
- *Potential Action Steps* 113

Chapter 7: Nurturing Through High Expectations and Being Culturally Responsive **115**
- Words From a Principal 116
- Words From a Professor 117
- The Importance of High Expectations 118
- A Safe and Nurturing Environment 120
- Culturally Responsive Practices 125
- Words From a Principal 128
- Conclusion 129
- Questions for Reflection and Discussion 129
- *Nurturing Through High Expectations Reflection* 130
- *Potential Action Steps* 131

Chapter 8: Building and Sustaining School Culture
and Maximizing Partnerships **133**
    Words From a Principal 133
    Words From a Professor 135
    School Culture 136
    Partnerships 139
    Conclusion 141
    Questions for Reflection and Discussion 141
    CRASEL Leadership Reflection 142
    Potential Action Steps 143

Epilogue **145**

References and Resources **147**

Index **155**

About the Authors

Dawn Brooks DeCosta, EdD, is the deputy superintendent of Harlem Community School District 5 in Harlem, New York City, where she leads the district's Culturally Responsive and Affirming Social-Emotional Leadership and Learning framework. She is the former principal of Thurgood Marshall Academy Lower School, where she focused her leadership on cultural responsiveness, social-emotional learning, and academic achievement. Dawn began her service of teaching in 1994, worked as a teacher for New York City public schools in Harlem for sixteen years, and served as principal for eleven years. Before that, she taught at St. Gabriel's Catholic School in East Elmhurst, Queens, New York.

Dawn's awards and recognitions include Teacher of the Year 1998, the Heroes of Education Award 2002 for her work with students after the September 11, 2001, tragedy, and Outstanding Educator 2002. She is a 2015 Yale Institute Marvin Mauer Spotlight Award winner and a 2015 Cahn Fellow with Teachers College, Columbia University. Dawn's dissertation, "Black Principal Perspectives on SEL and CRSL in Urban Schools: The Role of Beliefs, Values and Leadership Practices," was completed in 2020. Her research has appeared in *The Journal of Folklore and Education*, *Educator's Voice*, *Voices in Urban Education*, and

Comparative Education. Her chapter, "Restoring the Village Through Radical Self-Care," appeared in the book *From Being Woke to Doing the Work* in 2023.

Dawn holds a bachelor's in education from St. John's University in Queens, New York City, a master's in fine art education from Queens College, and a doctorate in education and a master's in educational leadership from Teachers College, Columbia University.

Mark Anthony Gooden, PhD, is Christian Johnson Endeavor Professor in Education Leadership at Teachers College, Columbia University. His research focuses broadly on culturally responsive school leadership, with specific interests in principalship, antiracist leadership, urban educational leadership, and legal issues in education. Before entering higher education, Mark served as a secondary mathematics teacher and departmental chair in Columbus Public Schools in Ohio and later as an assistant professor at the University of Cincinnati, where he also directed several leadership programs for seven years. He later served as the Margie Gurley Seay Centennial Professor of Education at the University of Texas at Austin and as director of the principalship program for nearly nine years.

Mark is former president of the University Council for Educational Administration (UCEA), a consortium of over one hundred higher education institutions committed to advancing the preparation and practice of educational leaders. He is the 2017 recipient of the UCEA Jay D. Scribner Mentoring Award and 2021 recipient of the UCEA Master Professor Award for distinguished service in teaching, curriculum development, and student mentoring. He coauthored *Five Practices for Equity-Focused School Leadership*. His research has appeared in *American Educational Research Journal, Educational Administration Quarterly, Teachers College Record, The Journal of Negro Education* & *Urban Education, Review of Educational Research, Educational Leadership*, and *Education Week*, among others.

Mark has spent over two decades in higher education developing and teaching courses in culturally responsive leadership, race, law, and research methods. He has consulted with school districts, universities, and nonprofit organizations by designing and delivering professional development courses and workshops in antiracist leadership, law, and community building. He earned his bachelor's degree in mathematics from Albany State University in Georgia (a Historically Black University) and his master's degree in mathematics education, as well as a second master's degree and a PhD in policy and leadership, from Ohio State University.

Introduction

What was the catalyst that propelled you into school leadership? When did you first feel the weight of personal responsibility and realize how challenging it would be? What drives you to keep pushing forward, and what wakes you up in the middle of the night? These are the questions most K–12 school leaders can answer easily, because being a school leader, with its inherent challenges, becomes part of your identity. Yet, with all the struggles of leadership, there are so many bright moments, valuable relationships, and inspiring experiences that allow us to continue the work. If you are searching for ways to lead your school through an approach that considers the student holistically, meeting not only their social-emotional needs but also their cultural needs, this book will provide the tools and resources your school community needs to build your individual and collective capacities.

This book is about culturally responsive and affirming social-emotional leadership (CRASEL), which combines the work of social-emotional learning (SEL) and culturally responsive school leadership (CRSL). It is a liberatory approach to leading and learning that raises racial and cultural self-awareness and sets high expectations while meeting the unique needs of the community. The approach aims to accomplish this while attending to students' individual and collective social and emotional needs through encouraging agency, social justice, voice, compassion, empathy, and positive relationship building. Leaders using this approach serve as lead learners in their own self-reflective process. Doing so includes engaging with a coach, mentor, critical friend, or thought partner along with members of the school community as they reflect, learn, develop a vision, and implement SEL and CRSL practices concurrently. Instead of an individualistic approach, this book proposes a collaborative method, as each member of the school community develops their individual capacities, at the same time building their team's strength by creating a supportive and caring school environment.

Being an educator, if done in the true advocacy of students and families, is being an activist. Those who hold the lives of students in their hands and seek a brighter future operate in a constant state of protest, pushing against and working through a system that marginalizes our most vulnerable. The divisive political climate in the United States has impacted the views around SEL and CRSL across the country. Fear and misinformation regarding the intent of these researched frameworks have caused undue restrictions on their integration in schools, despite their proven benefit throughout school communities. Students, staff, and families therefore suffer without strategies and practices that foster a culture in which everyone is seen and heard, where communities of care prevent bullying and disparate disciplinary policy, where students feel a sense of belonging, and where they experience support through emotional struggles.

In this changing educational environment, we have a powerful window of opportunity to educate, enhance, and refine learning experiences for our students. By integrating these practices, we can help school communities thrive, care, question, innovate, know themselves, show compassion and empathy, and ultimately change the trajectory toward a more just society. This work is beneficial to all students, of every background, race, and ethnicity.

This book is a collaboration between research professor Mark Anthony Gooden and practitioner and former principal Dawn Brooks DeCosta. Mark's research focuses broadly on culturally responsive school leadership with specific interests in principalship, antiracist leadership, urban educational leadership, and legal issues in education. Dawn served as principal of Thurgood Marshall Academy Lower School (TMALS), a model school focused on academic excellence, cultural responsiveness, SEL, social justice, student agency, and family engagement, and is currently deputy superintendent of Harlem Public Schools. You'll read our thoughts on and experiences with each chapter's topic in the recurring sections Words From a Principal, written by Dawn, and Words From a Professor, written by Mark.

Our goal with this book is to support you by providing the following.

- An overview of the foundation of and research on SEL, CRSL, and CRASEL
- Real-world examples of the practices in action from a school leader's perspective
- Insight on the perspectives of members of the school community
- A thought process to use with a coach, mentor, critical friend, or thought partner
- Reflective discussion questions to answer throughout the journey, from building knowledge to implementation

This book also highlights Dawn's experiences as a school leader at TMALS. Each chapter features a personal story about the challenges and successes she encountered in co-creating with her community a school culture centered in culturally responsive SEL. Here, we provide a little more background on TMALS and how we will use it as an example in this book.

Dawn was a leader of color in a school population that is 95 percent students of color and a staff predominantly of color. Although her context is that of a school leader working in a predominantly Black community, the experiences, the strategies, and the lessons she shares are applicable in many contexts. The demographics and culture of TMALS may be very different from yours. However, we assert that there is learning, relevance, and worth in the Black context that readers from all cultures can apply to their own contexts. The experiences of building self-awareness, authentically connecting to students and families, and creating a culture of care centered on belonging can be universally beneficial to all learning institutions, regardless of the learning community's demographic. At the heart of schools, the most vibrant, engaging learning environments are those that hold a sense of community where *all* members of that community are valued. At the same time, these schools nurture connectedness and belonging, and the community also learns about the value of all of humanity and their connection to it.

As you read Dawn's words in each chapter, consider the ways in which her experiences at TMALS can benefit you and your school's pursuit to build relationships and authentic connections that benefit all students, staff, and families within and beyond the school walls.

Words From a Principal

The opportunity to teach at TMALS gave me a chance to tie my values to a mission that aligned with my identity, my cultural values, and my aspirations for myself and the Black community. Named for Thurgood Marshall, the first Black Supreme Court justice, TMALS opened in 2005 in a collaboration between the Harlem community, Abyssinian Development Corporation, New Visions for Public Schools, and the New York City Department of Education (NYC DOE). TMALS is the vision of the world-renowned Harlem pastor of Abyssinian Baptist Church and community and social justice leader Dr. Calvin O. Butts III. The late Dr. Butts created the school to fill a gap in the corridor of learning that he envisioned. Our school is grounded in academic excellence, cultural awareness and relevance, self-esteem, and the arts.

At the Summer Principals Academy at Teachers College, Columbia University, under the program director Dr. Craig Richards, I was exposed to the world of self-awareness and mindfulness. The leadership program that I entered, initially only to further advance my degree in education, unexpectedly inspired me to lead. I transitioned into the role of principal of TMALS and, influenced by Teachers College's coursework of mindful practice, emotional intelligence, and self-awareness, I embarked on integrating these practices into the school's mission and educational experience.

The mission of TMALS began with the proverb "It takes a village to raise a child." Through a commitment to collective greatness, growth, and uplifting our students, more than fifteen years after our inception, our mission now states, "We are the village that raises the child." My experience from TMALS, documented throughout this book, shows how schools can provide rich learning opportunities that encourage students to connect with social justice actions, understand the history of activism, question oppression, and feel empowerment and agency. The school aims to do this while attending to the emotional and holistic needs of not only the students, but also caregivers, teachers, staff, and the larger community. This endeavor is always a work in progress.

I wrote this book with the collaboration, support, and guidance of my mentor in culturally responsive school leadership, Dr. Mark Anthony Gooden. I began learning about Dr. Gooden's work during my doctoral studies at Teachers College, when he was leading and teaching in the Education Leadership Program. Through my time in the program and beyond, Dr. Gooden has provided professional development, support, and coaching for me as a school leader, as he does for leaders across the United States. Being a lifelong learner in this work while grounding myself in research has been key to the success of TMALS. Leaders must lead, and leaders must continually learn. It was at Mark's encouragement that we tell the story of the work being done at TMALS, and the successes, challenges, and perseverance needed in the work.

About This Book

This book will share the CRASEL framework so you can begin to execute a culturally responsive approach grounded in SEL in your school communities. This framework was developed through research, experiences, successes, obstacles, trials, and errors. Our goal is to help you take the leap in engaging in the work needed to create school cultures and practices that uplift, educate, nurture, and support students. Through a holistic approach, we can meet not only students' social and emotional needs, but also their need to become more aware of their identities, histories, and perspectives as well as those of diverse cultures.

Chapter 1 introduces CRSL and SEL using research-based frameworks that describe the benefits of both approaches on student success and school culture.

Chapter 2 explains how to bridge SEL and culturally responsive leadership in a way that attends to the social and emotional, as well as cultural, needs of students, staff, and families. We describe CRASEL, a combined approach that we explore further in the rest of the book.

Chapter 3 shows how you, as school leader and lead learner, must model self-care and vulnerability to guide and support your school community in this work.

Chapter 4 goes deeper into the work of self-awareness and engages you in a racial autobiography, as well as other tools for racial reflection, that you can share with your school communities.

Chapter 5 offers practical strategies for creating strong relationships in your school community and the trust and healing you need to engage in CRASEL work.

Chapter 6 shares the importance of advocacy and tells how you can be an advocate for your school community, helping your students and community members advocate for themselves and what they care about.

Chapter 7 shows how you can use research-based best practices, article studies, and professional development to learn about your community and encourage high expectations in your students.

Chapter 8 describes the collaborative effort and focus on community and school culture you need to sustain the work.

Each chapter features vignettes, frameworks, protocols, self-reflection and discussion questions, and strategies. At the end of each chapter are opportunities for self-reflection or discussion. Some of the questions are personal and are most applicable for individual use. You can also use this text for a team book study to promote collaborative thought partnering as leaders learn and grow in these practices in support of one another.

At the end of each chapter, a "Potential Action Steps" reproducible helps you consider which actions you and your school community are ready to embark on. You don't need to use these in sequence but can choose the best fit for your school. Additionally, consider that the time commitment within each potential action step will vary. Some of the action steps can happen within days, and others may take months of consistent practice.

We wrote this book with the hope of inspiring other school leaders and communities to join together with compassion and bravery to engage in this most meaningful work—not only for the benefit of all students, staff, and families, but also for our future and society at large. Leaders cannot work effectively in isolation. It takes a whole village, each of us bringing our expertise, perspectives, unique talents, gifts, hands, minds, and hearts to envision and create a true culture of care that centers itself in both CRSL and SEL. Our goal in sharing this work is to advance needed change in school communities toward systems of strong positive relationships of belonging, nurturing, agency, and care that allow those communities to flourish culturally, academically, socially, and emotionally. This is the change we want to see!

Questions for Reflection and Discussion

1. What is your school community like, and how is that connected to your identity?
2. What do you find most exciting about working with the students in your community?
3. What is a barrier to doing your best work in your school?
4. What do you need to know and be able to do to become a better leader for your school and community?

1

Understanding Social-Emotional Learning and Culturally Responsive School Leadership

In this chapter, we introduce two practices that are fundamental to our educational mission: social-emotional learning (SEL) and culturally responsive school leadership (CRSL). We will also explore the research that supports the practices and explain how you can implement these practices to positively impact your school's climate, culture, and learning environment.

Words From a Principal

When I became a school leader, I spent my entire first year crying with everyone who was in crisis. When students were in distress with a conflict, I cried with them. When teachers came to my office crying about a classroom incident, I cried with them. When a parent came to me, crying about their life struggles and parenting challenges, I cried with them. I felt powerless to help fight the root of many of the challenges, often poverty and systemic racism.

The weight of carrying everyone's emotions and wanting to fix every problem began to wear on my own emotional state. Leading in an urban environment with increasing poverty and systemically racist accountability measures at times felt like an unbearably heavy burden. The isolation of leadership and the need to fight against measures that didn't reflect our successes often left me feeling abandoned, alone, and like a failure. I was drained and depleted, and I knew that, physically and emotionally, I couldn't continue at that pace. There had to be a better way for all of us in the school community to better manage our daily stresses, and in ways that would create a culture of care and support in which we all had the tools we needed to recognize our own emotions and the effect our emotions and actions had on others. We needed a strategy for expressing emotions and ways to show compassion for ourselves and others along with the tools to practice self-care as a school community. SEL is not only for students, but also for the adults supporting them.

Words From a Professor

In an Educational Administration Quarterly *article (Gooden, 2005), I wrote about Thomas Grant, an African American principal who had returned to his alma mater to lead. His alma mater was in a predominantly Black community with a large percentage of working-class people of lower socioeconomic status. While it was apparent that Grant was a very capable leader—adroit at engaging interpersonally, bringing teachers together around a mandate, motivating and supporting students, and managing conflict—he was also good at something else. And this "something else" was his most powerful ability: empathy.*

Grant used empathy as a fierce driver of equity-focused leadership. His story intimately connected him to the community's emotional needs and academic aspirations, and he carried this narrative deep in his heart, revealing it when necessary.

While Grant may not have expressed his compassion as openly or frequently as Dawn in her first year, he most certainly demonstrated a true love for his students and regularly remarked about the inequitable and tough situations they were often expected to overcome with minimal support. He followed what was called at the time an ethno-humanist and bureaucrat model of leading *(Lomotey, 1989; Lomotey & Weiler, 2021). Though Grant's skills enabled him to succeed at the traditional notions of leadership that any capable and motivated leader could learn, he implemented a social-emotional and culturally sound response through three qualities relating directly to his students and their well-being: compassion for his students, confidence in their ability to achieve, and a commitment to their well-being and their community that did its best to support them. Grant pulled together these components to demonstrate a kind of open vulnerability that some leaders may struggle with in their own SEL journeys. Though Grant worked hard to ensure he was emotionally present for his students and staff, I wonder if he had enough time to practice self-care as a leader in a demanding principalship.*

> **RELATE AND REFLECT**
> - Can you relate to Dawn's experience of feeling emotionally overwhelmed while supporting her school community? How so?
> - What are some ways you practice self-care?
> - If you don't currently have a practice, what are some activities you enjoy that restore you emotionally?

Social-Emotional Learning

We as teachers have heard that SEL is good for all students. But what is SEL really? Where did the concept originate, what proof do we have that it's a good practice, and what does it look like when it's done well? SEL has become a common catchphrase often used to entice leaders to purchase shiny programs and products. SEL is woven, albeit sometimes superficially, into several accountability measures, such as school leader and teacher evaluations and school quality measures.

The Collaborative for Academic, Social, and Emotional Learning (CASEL, n.d.) defines *social and emotional learning* as follows.

> Social and emotional learning (SEL) is the process through which children and adults acquire and effectively apply the knowledge, attitudes, and skills necessary to understand and manage emotions, set and achieve positive goals, feel and show empathy for others, establish and maintain positive relationships, and make responsible decisions.

Origins

In the 1960s, James P. Comer, an African American researcher at Yale, began his work investigating students' experiences and the impact of relationships on their academic achievement (Comer & Gates, 2004). His goal was to determine whether the holistic nurturing of the student through positive, supportive relationships between students, staff, and parents would positively impact their academic achievement. His research pilot, which he called the Comer Process, influenced what would later be known as SEL. Comer's work created a gateway for other researchers, organizations, and policies that allowed SEL to emerge

(Durlak, Domitrovich, Weissberg, & Gullotta, 2015; Moreno, Nagasawa, & Schwartz, 2019).

The concept of SEL interfaces with emotional intelligence. Peter Salovey and John D. Mayer (1990a) coined the term *emotional intelligence*, describing it as "a form of social intelligence that involves the ability to monitor one's own and other's feelings and emotions, to discriminate among them, and to use this information to guide one's thinking and action" (p. 5). In 2020, Dawn added the following ideas.

> [Emotional intelligence] is described as not only a recognition of one's emotions and the emotions of others, but also a set of cognitive abilities. These cognitive abilities are specifically seen when presented with emotion-based problems to solve—hence, the increased ability to function in work and school environments where problem solving is a regular occurrence. (Brooks DeCosta, 2020, p. 37)

First defined by psychologist Daniel Goleman (2006) and expounded on by Yale social psychologists Marc A. Brackett, Susan E. Rivers, and Peter Salovey (2011), the skills of emotional intelligence include recognizing and regulating emotions, proactively solving problems, and displaying compassion while building positive relationships with others. Researchers Jessica D. Hoffmann, Zorana Ivcevic, and Marc A. Brackett's (2018) work further emphasizes that instruction in emotional intelligence improves students' social skills.

Engaging students in building their emotional intelligence skills requires that educators create an environment of expression and agency. Without the opportunity to express their emotions, talk through challenges, share their perceptions, and interrogate their beliefs, students are not able to build and strengthen their emotional intelligence. In many cases, after a strong foundation is built, teachers need to step into the role of facilitator, where developmentally appropriate, to allow students the opportunity to use and practice their emotional intelligence.

The CASEL Framework

As we've established, educators and child development psychologists developed the concept of SEL by combining the tenets of emotional intelligence with other life skills. The CASEL framework was created by a group of leading scholars in various fields such as child development, education, and emotional intelligence in 1994, and is widely used as the basis for many SEL programs, policies, and practices (CASEL, n.d.).

The five tenets of the CASEL framework are (1) self-awareness, (2) self-management, (3) social awareness, (4) relationship skills, and (5) responsible decision making (CASEL, n.d.). It's important for educators and leaders to not only teach these skills in the classroom, but also model them in their interactions with students, parents, and colleagues. Much of effective teaching and leading is modeling. This is also true for SEL. School psychologists Kyongboon Kwon, Amanda R. Hanrahan, and Kevin A. Kupzyk (2017) find a connection between maladaptive student behavior and problems with emotion regulation. This further solidifies the impact of SEL on a student's ability to function in a learning environment.

Students who experience life challenges such as economic disadvantages, housing discrimination, racism, foster care, arrests and incarceration, and food and physical insecurity may still appear resilient. However, these life experiences can adversely affect their emotional well-being, impacting their relationships, their self-concept, and ultimately their ability to find academic success in school (Burroughs & Barkauskas, 2017; Greenberg, Domitrovich, Weissberg, & Durlak, 2017). Students who may present as disengaged, withdrawn, or resistant must be supported socially and emotionally in developmentally appropriate ways. The end goal of SEL in the classroom should be to ensure that students feel a sense of belonging and connection that allows them to engage in learning, collaborate effectively with peers, and persevere through academic challenges.

The COVID-19 pandemic and the emotional impact of isolation on students prompted many school districts to require that SEL become a priority component of curriculum and approaches to support. Without appropriate training, coaching, and support, however, many efforts toward integrating SEL can become shallow and inauthentic. You must dig deep, investigate, research, and observe effective models before committing to integrate a given practice into a school.

SEL for the Educator

Research literature suggests that the teacher is the most important factor in teaching SEL in schools (Oliveira, Roberto, Pereira, Marques-Pinto, & Veiga-Simão, 2021). This indicates the need for teachers and leaders to engage in their own personal work with emotional intelligence and SEL to best support students. Some of the exercises in this book may feel very personal, but they ultimately have the potential to expand your efforts into powerful SEL work in the school setting.

Leaders should set the standard for engaging in social-emotional work and personally revealing exercises, even though doing so might make them feel vulnerable and open to criticism. However, they should acknowledge why they are doing so, help others see the benefits, and finally inspire and encourage them to do the same. Being a model in social-emotional work can increase the empathy of all involved and remind the staff that the real reason for engaging in this powerful educational work is to enlighten students as learners, expose them to the power of education in a democratic society, and give them access to tools that will improve the quality of their lives and their community members. Chapter 3 (page 53) will provide more guidance on how to address teachers' SEL needs.

Words From a Principal

I regularly have a morning meeting with the students after they eat breakfast. One morning, while sharing our moods—a crucial part of our daily SEL work—one of my fifth graders raised his hand and said, "I'm in the red." He was indicating his emotional level on the Mood Meter, a chart we use to identify and express our emotional states; red connotates high energy and low pleasantness (see figure 1.1, page 25). He said he felt angry but also sad.

When I asked why he felt that way, he described an incident the day before where he had a bad experience in a store. He was made to feel "less than" by a worker in the store. The student began to cry while we all stood together, about a hundred of us standing together and looking at him while we listened to his story. The boy told us the story through his tears. I could hear the pride and the love in his voice as he described how his father stood up for him. And in the words I heard the love this father had for his son and the familiarity he had with this type of experience. And the question the boy had for me and all of us was, "What I want to know is . . . why do they hate us?"

For me, this and other conversations like this are clear examples of why SEL on its own is not enough. It would not have been enough for me to say, "I'm sorry that happened to you, and I hope you feel better." There was something this student needed at that moment that called for more. The conversation we had as a community that morning after his question had to address racism, discrimination, and at the same time self-love, determination, perseverance, and a way to move forward while sadly our children also experience and feel the hatred of racism.

> **RELATE AND REFLECT**
> - Can you envision another way to support this student through this experience as well as those students who were listening?
> - Can you relate to the experience of trying to support students through difficult experiences? How?
> - What connections can you make with your own experiences and creating a culture of care and community that supports one another?

SEL Benefits and Limitations

The following sections offer some ways SEL can help us handle challenging situations like the one Dawn described. We will look at how SEL can be beneficial in building trust, helping us have difficult conversations, fighting invisibility syndrome, and other challenges students face—with some caveats.

SEL Builds Trust in the Face of Trauma

Students experience an overload of technological information. Through social media, gaming, and varied information platforms, they are bombarded with negative images. Many of these images can be traumatizing if students are not developmentally ready to unpack or identify what they're seeing. As adults, we can barely manage the violence we witness, if not in our own neighborhoods, then on the news and through social media. How confusing and traumatizing is it for students to digest these images without the proper context or developmental readiness to manage what they are taking in? SEL can support them in regulating the effects of trauma by providing tools and strategies for self-awareness, relationship building, emotion regulation, stress reduction, and other coping mechanisms, thereby allowing students who have experienced trauma a path to thriving academically.

Students can experience stress due to occurrences and challenges that may happen naturally in day-to-day expectations and interactions with others in and out of school. Trauma presents as a lasting impact on the emotions and mental health of a student due to a highly stressful, terrifying, violent, or painful event or series of events. The impact of trauma and stress on students' social and emotional well-being can include depression, suicide, suicidal ideation, low self-esteem, fear, anxiety, and poor relationships with teachers and peers (Brooks DeCosta, 2020). Additionally, teacher misinterpretations of a student's emotional state, life circumstances, and ability to regulate can also lead to inordinate referrals to special education.

A child's exposure to violence has a direct impact on their social and emotional well-being. Child development experts Amanda J. Moreno, Mark K. Nagasawa, and Toby Schwartz (2019) identify the effects of repeated violence on a child's sense of safety, which they need for their holistic development. Post-traumatic stress disorder (PTSD) specialists Jani Nöthling, Sharain Suliman, Lindi Martin, Candice Simmons, and Soraya Seedat (2019) define the lasting influence of community violence on children as PTSD, where they encounter sleep disturbances and other physiological reactions.

However, SEL without context can do students more harm than good. Consider the emotional support of students who directly or indirectly experience racial injustice, and the validity of their anger, anxiety, and confusion. These students should be encouraged to express—not suppress—those feelings. In this case, the regulation of those valid feelings may be to allow students to *express*, rather than *calm*, those feelings so they might go away. Students' experiences and sociopolitical context should be considered, and support provided as they experience their variety of valid emotions. Students should be given the opportunity to express emotions freely and in ways that allow them an outlet that will not cause additional harm and supports them through those emotions.

In an interview, SEL scholar and practitioner Dena Simmons explains that without the proper context and consideration of the realities of students' experiences of systemic racism, we risk SEL becoming "white supremacy with a hug" (Madda, 2019). The SEL concept has been incorrectly used to police and control the behavior and expression of Black and Brown students, which can cause more harm and trauma. Instead of allowing expression and agency and an understanding of the life circumstances of all students and the valid impact on their emotions, those who are unaware of the research behind SEL and its proper use may unintentionally minimize the validity of a student's emotions. In misinterpreting an emotion or the source of that emotion, educators can respond in ways that not only inadequately address the student's needs but also cause lasting harm and mistrust. SEL requires trust and cultural responsiveness, but many SEL approaches neglect to adequately and explicitly identify the connections.

SEL Helps Us Have Difficult Conversations About Systemic Racism

SEL's component of self-awareness and the journey to self-reflection are needed prior to engaging in conversations about race. Investigating our experiences and beliefs that impact our perspectives on race is crucial so we are not blindly engaging in these conversations without understanding our own impact. SEL's self-management and our awareness of how we affect others are also key, as is the social awareness of the life experiences of ourselves and others and their impact on our emotions, actions, and perspectives.

SEL alone does not confront the injustices and inequities that students face. In some instances, SEL may conflict with injustices and inequities. Culturally responsive scholar-practitioners Jemimah L. Young, Jamaal R. Young, and Bettie Ray Butler (2018) note that Black students have been historically marginalized through school discipline policies that function "at the very heart of several negative outcomes (e.g., bad grades, retention, recidivism, incarceration, economic hardship, etc.)" (p. 97).

Unfortunately, some schools use SEL to police and control student behavior, with strategies to "calm down" and regulate emotions. This is avoidance of doing the most difficult work that SEL calls us to do, if we truly wish to be culturally responsive. In an unjust society, antiracism requires not that we calm down, but instead that we channel that anger and express justifiable outrage while demanding change. SEL should promote expression, not stifle it.

Simmons (2019b) notes that racism and true SEL cannot coexist in schools who say they are committed to SEL and practice policies that are inherently racist. In his article "Antiracism in Social-Emotional Learning: Why It's Not Enough to Talk the Talk," Tony Weaver Jr. (2020) says, "We can't tell . . . kids to take 10 deep breaths when people who look like them are dying because they can't breathe." SEL, implemented in the proper way, however, and sensitive to the context of the lives of students and the systemic racism they experience daily, can assist with the emotional strength needed to engage in difficult conversations about race. We want to emphasize that students of color and White students are all experiencing racism, even though schools tend to teach White students to ignore it. Research scholars Michalinos Zembylas and Cheryl E. Matias (2023) discuss how teacher preparedness programs teach educators to ignore race, further emphasizing structures where Whiteness is centered as the standard.

> *In an unjust society, antiracism requires not that we calm down, but instead that we channel that anger and express justifiable outrage while demanding change.*

The movement against teaching about racism in school centers on the idea that White children should not be made to feel uncomfortable about such topics. What is not considered is the consistent discomfort of Black students in those spaces where an uncomfortable, traumatizing history is ignored and revised so White students can feel comfortable. Black history is American history; therefore, all students should receive the true knowledge of the history of this country, including its successes and achievements, as well as the challenges and traumatic events that brought us to where we are today.

SEL Fights Invisibility Syndrome

When used with an equity-centered approach, SEL can help students feel seen and heard. Through recognizing the varied life experiences of diverse students, their impact, and the opportunities schools can provide students to express those emotions, SEL can promote visibility and inclusion.

To truly support their needs, it is necessary to affirm our students as whole, multifaceted people. Students who are not seen and affirmed culturally, socially, and emotionally can develop a sense of invisibility in their classrooms and school community, leaving them marginalized. Psychologists Anderson J. Franklin, Nancy Boyd-Franklin, and Shalonda Kelly (2006) describe *invisibility syndrome* as a result of "cumulative experiences of confronting race-related stress, emotional abuse, and the psychological trauma of racism" (p. 13).

In *Pedagogy of the Oppressed*, his landmark work of liberationist education, Paulo Freire (2018, original work published 1968) defines *suboppression* as the ways in which one who has been oppressed internalizes the oppression, or oppresses others. Franklin and colleagues (2006) agree that children can internalize the oppression they experience.

> When young people practice suboppression in this way, they do not have their own worldview because they are instead experiencing their oppressor's psychological violence in the most intimate of ways, conforming to their oppression, as embodied in how they move through the world on a day-to-day, minute-to-minute basis. (p. 12)

Microaggressions are the subtle, intended or unintended acts of bias, including discriminatory comments, gestures, and insults, that can have lasting impact. Repeated microaggressions can result in trauma for the child, resulting in a diminished self-concept.

If we are to prepare active citizens who stand for justice and stand against racism, we must teach students the realities of unjust systems, so they are able to recognize injustices and oppression and fight against such policies and practices as adults. It is imperative that White educators connect emotionally and with bravery to disrupting racism through one of the most powerful tools we have: education.

Simmons (2019b) explains that SEL requires that educators ground their approach in their sociopolitical context. She advocates that however uncomfortable conversations about race can be, it is essential that antiracist educators are courageous and confront the inequities that exist in their own classrooms and school environments, whether the population is Black and Brown or predominantly White. Our students' experiences are unique, and SEL requires that we are authentic, trustworthy, and brave enough to acknowledge what our students are experiencing. We also must provide them the safe spaces they need to express their truths and support them in maintaining their emotional wellness. Part of supporting students through indirect and direct experiences of racial trauma, which can include repeatedly viewing racial violence through the media, is to provide them a platform to express their emotions, validate those emotions, and allow them to see their own power to enact change through their own spheres of influence. Acts of social justice and learning about ways in which people actively fight injustices can empower students to envision the possibilities for change. This can provide healing and combat invisibility syndrome.

Culturally Responsive School Leadership

Professors Muhammad A. Khalifa, Mark Anthony Gooden, and James Earl Davis (2016) define *CRSL* as the culturally responsive beliefs, behaviors, and actions of school leaders. Their CRSL framework includes four main areas in which the leader does the following.

1. Critically self reflects on leadership behaviors
2. Develops culturally responsive teachers
3. Promotes culturally responsive and inclusive school environments
4. Engages students, parents, and local contexts

This framework is based on a literature review that begins with definitions given by Gloria Ladson-Billings and Geneva Gay, the scholars who coined the phrases *culturally relevant pedagogy* and *culturally responsive pedagogy*, respectively. Ladson-Billings's (1995a) definition of what is culturally relevant contains three core components: academic success, cultural competence, and critical consciousness. She asserts that "all students can and must succeed" (p. 163). Gay (2002) defines culturally responsive pedagogy as "using the cultural characteristics, experiences, and perspectives of ethnically diverse students as conduits for teaching them more effectively" (p. 106).

A culturally responsive approach emanates from a culture of interpersonal care. Tom Cavanagh, Angus Macfarlane, Ted Glynn, and Sonja Macfarlane (2012) describe how a:

> Culture of care requires schools and teachers to be cognizant of how the school and classroom values, beliefs and practices make it safe for all students to engage, to contribute, to belong and to feel confident in their own cultural identities. (p. 443)

This concept of care is also central to SEL. Rosa L. Rivera-McCutchen (2021), associate professor at CUNY Lehman College, notes that the heart of radical care in school leadership is holding an antiracist stance. This quality of leadership maintains high expectations; sees the highest potential in the school community; builds trusting, authentic relationships; and works collaboratively toward a collective goal. These leaders are transformational forces in their school communities.

Transformational Leaders

It is important to note that a culturally responsive culture of care cannot happen systematically in a school without the school leader's full support and participation. Expectations for schoolwide systems and the accountability for implementing, observing, and supporting those systems rest with you, the school leader. Although it is essential, as we will explain in later chapters, to work collaboratively and build the capacity and leadership in teachers, students, and parents, the driving force is you, the school leader. Without your active role in creating a culturally responsive environment, the work may happen in pockets but will not happen systematically within the school.

Without the school leader's active role in creating a culturally responsive environment, the work may happen in pockets but will not happen systematically within the school.

A school is not culturally responsive unless students can experience high expectations and affirmation of diverse cultures in every part of the school building and in every class they attend. The work can be easily undone if all adults in the building are not onboard. Schoolwide staff buy-in and commitment are worthy goals to push for and work toward. You are central to driving the school community to capture these positive ways of being for our schools. Jess R. Weiler and Kofi Lomotey (2022) encourage school leadership preparation programs to "not only provide an understanding of the present systemic inequities and develop the skills of organizational transformation," but also "show how it can be done in the face of resistance from those who benefit from and hold tight to the status quo" (p. 122).

Gail Furman (2012) notes that the leader who centers social justice is "action oriented and transformative, committed and persistent, inclusive and democratic, relational and caring, reflective, and oriented toward a socially just pedagogy" (p. 195). Through a culturally responsive approach to school policies, systems, and curricula, leaders can center the diverse identities of the students in their learning. In combining that approach with one that also acknowledges students' sociocultural experiences in the support of their social and emotional development, you can create a culture of care. In collaboration with educators and families, the culture of care should be present in all aspects of students' experiences at school, including expectations for their interactions with peers and adults, and the perceived relationships students observe between adults at the school.

Transformational leadership is characterized by leadership behaviors such as modeling secure values and open-mindedness, inspiring others with a creative disposition, communicating high expectations, and exercising compassion for those they lead through a positive vision (Arnold, 2017). There is an increasing need for school leaders to inhabit the transformational, culturally responsive leadership skills that allow them to meet the unique sociopolitical needs of today's students (Horsford, Grosland, & Gunn, 2011).

The transformational leader is willing to advocate for their communities and challenge practices and policies that marginalize their students and families. In an environment of high accountability around student performance measures, a leader who centers students' social-emotional needs must find creative ways to meet those needs while navigating the demands of data and compliance. It can be challenging to balance accountability expectations with those that focus on the care of students. Being accountable for test scores and student academic performance can lead you to become laser focused on academic achievement. However, "a narrow focus on accountability, excellence, and achievement cannot be maintained while ignoring what children are experiencing emotionally and socially if students' academic success and performance in schools are expected to increase" (Brooks DeCosta, 2020, p. 48).

The transformational leader is a role model of the practice they wish to implement. Modeling cultural responsiveness and social-emotional support in their leadership of adults is as important as the model they present for students. A leader who exhibits compassion even in instances of evaluation and supervision can inspire those they lead to incorporate the practices with their students. Leaders can model CRSL and SEL as they co-create policies and systems and navigate challenges for the school community.

The adults in the building should reflect the culture of care in their interactions and relationships with students. You set the tone for this behavior. Students can learn more effectively in a culture of care, where they feel safe and cared for. Staff members also need a sense of safety and care if they are to flourish in their roles. Both staff and students need to feel a positive self-concept to persevere through challenges. It is therefore worth it, for those who push academic achievement, that SEL and culturally responsive practices create the learning environment where students and educators can thrive.

RELATE AND REFLECT
- How are all students made to feel emotionally safe in your school? How are staff made to feel emotionally safe in your school?
- How are educators in your school encouraged to be empathetic and compassionate, and to support the development of empathy in students?
- How do you model a culture of care in your style of leadership?

An SEL Approach Centered in Cultural Responsiveness

This section includes daily actions leaders and educators can take in implementing an SEL approach centered in cultural responsiveness. Each school community is different, and their readiness for these practices can vary, so start small and expand according to your school community's needs and readiness. This, as with everything, will take time to build. Allow your school community some grace in learning and implementing these practices. Some daily research-based routines and practices include the following.

- **Daily guided meditation, yoga, brain breaks, or self-awareness practices in all classrooms:** You can implement these practices schoolwide in a collaborative approach with staff. Consult with classroom teachers to determine where to include these mindfulness practices in the daily schedule. Once you've made a collective decision, document the school's chosen mindfulness practices in the schedule. You should actively support and monitor the consistency of these practices schoolwide and provide feedback to teachers when this practice is done well and with consistency. Teachers of specialized classes such as physical education, dance, or music should also implement these practices consistently where possible. Pure Edge (https://pureedgeinc.org) is a program for educators that provides training and free resources for yoga and brain breaks for classroom use. These practices can help students breathe, move, and rest to create focus and reduce stress and anxiety. Studies show that the benefits of mindfulness, yoga, and brain breaks help students self-regulate, build a positive self-concept, reduce stress, boost physical wellness, and develop the focus needed for academic performance (Wang & Hagins, 2016).

- **Student self-awareness leaders in all classrooms:** Once the adults are trained and prepared to implement the school's chosen practices and consistency is built and modeled for the students, there is an opportunity to promote student ownership, voice, and agency by appointing student leaders. The school community can decide what process to use to select student leaders. The student leaders should be trained to lead the chosen SEL practices and should have the opportunity to lead these practices in classrooms daily. The school should provide any needed resources to lead the practice. This can be done as early as kindergarten.

- **Culturally relevant imagery, texts, and artifacts in the school environment:** Ensure the school environment, including classroom libraries, reflects diverse images representing various races and ethnicities. Be sure the curriculum itself reflects various perspectives and points of view. The texts students engage with in the curriculum and in classroom libraries should represent characters of various races, cultures, and ethnicities to provide a diversity of thoughts, perspectives, and experiences. It is important for students to see themselves represented in the curriculum and texts they read. It is also important for them to see images of diverse races and cultures they may be unfamiliar with to broaden their knowledge and build connections.

- **Culturally responsive rituals and routines schoolwide:** Consider the practices, rituals, and routines that you can include to foster cultural responsiveness schoolwide. Some of those practices can occur in town halls, assemblies, classroom routines, and so on. Some of these culturally responsive rituals and routines include the following.
  - Community circles
  - Restorative circles
  - Call-and-response chants
  - Poetry recitations
  - Classroom names aligned with community landmarks, colleges, or cultural institutions

  Some of the culturally responsive instructional practices include the following.
  - High expectations
  - Growth mindsets
  - Academic talk structures and student-facilitated discussions
  - Schoolwide writing units reflecting culture, activism, and social justice
  - Student agency and voice
  - Actionable feedback to students, from students, and between students
  - Opportunities for students to make their thinking visible

- **The RULER approach:** The RULER approach is a program created by Marc Brackett, inspired by Peter Salovey and John Mayer's (1990a, 1990b) work in emotional intelligence. Brackett was also inspired by an SEL curriculum created by his uncle, Marvin Mauer. In collaboration with the Yale Center for Emotional Intelligence (YCEI), RULER is a program endorsed by CASEL. The name is an acronym of practices the RULER program supports: recognizing, understanding, labeling, expressing, and regulating emotions. It is a process that includes four anchor tools: the Charter, the Mood

Meter, the Meta-Moment, and the Blueprint. Each of the anchor tools includes practices for incorporating SEL into daily routines that encourage the RULER practices. YCEI (https://ycei.org) provides research, training, and resources for school staff. The Mood Meter, which Dawn refers to in some of her Words From a Principal sections, is shown in figure 1.1.

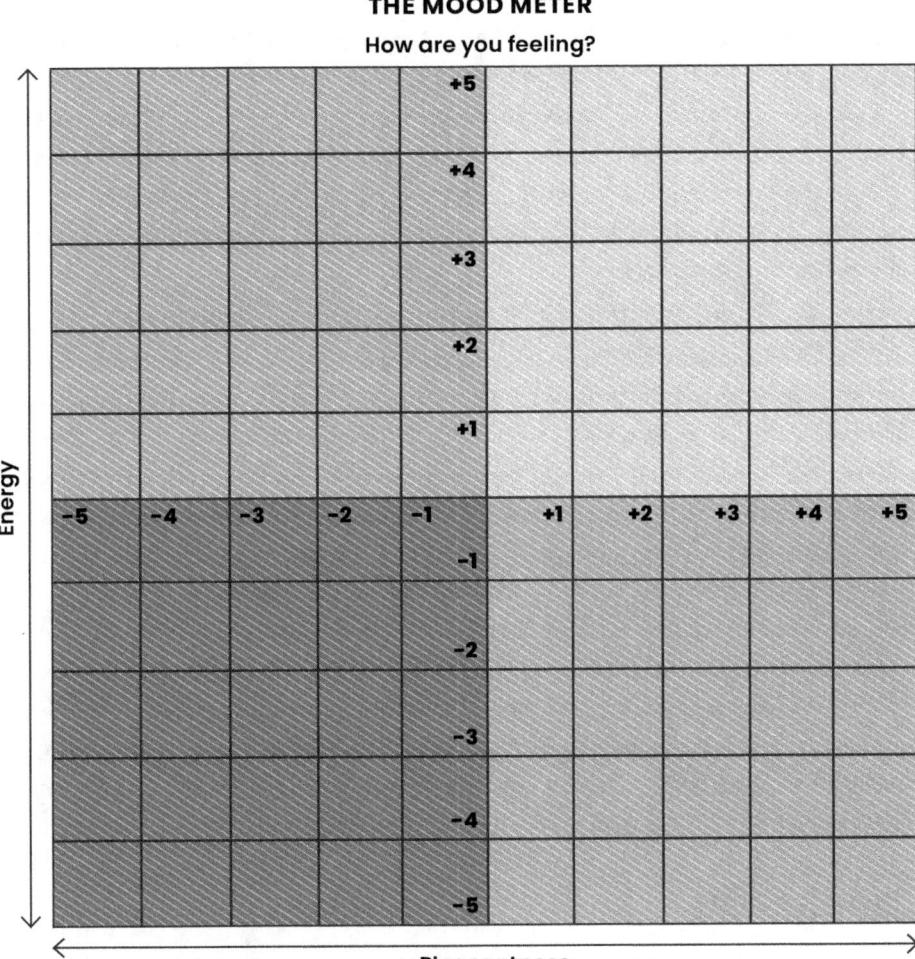

Source: *Yale Center for Emotional Intelligence (n.d.).*
Figure 1.1: The Mood Meter RULER tool.

This tool can help students improve their emotional intelligence skills by helping them better understand their feelings.

It is important that you build teacher leadership into daily SEL practices for sustainability. Recognize and highlight teachers who exhibit highly effective practices in SEL and let them serve as models or lab classrooms for one another and for new staff.

Words From a Principal

The practices at TMALS have evolved over the years. As noted in the introduction, the school began with the goal of emphasizing academic achievement, Black excellence, and social justice. Over the years, the vision has grown to include student agency, the arts, SEL, and mindful practices. The daily practices at the school are school community driven. The school's current mission and vision were co-created by the leaders, teachers, support staff, students, families, and long-standing community-based partners at the school.

My move to principal of TMALS was not an automatic integration. My very emotionally challenging first year as a school leader forced me to seek a better way of creating a more positive school community, and I was able to tap into what I had learned. What makes TMALS unique is its approach to SEL that is rooted and centered in antiracist and culturally responsive practices. The curriculum at TMALS, largely created and guided by the teachers, reflects the identity of the students through an antiracist social justice lens centered in SEL. Students learn about leaders of color who look like them to help build a positive self-concept while they also learn about diverse cultures and diverse perspectives on historical events. Student voice is elevated, and opportunities for students to interrogate discrimination and injustice in a real-world context are part of the curriculum. The belief in the students, the investment in nurturing their highest potential, their beauty, the value of their identity, their genius, and the depth of possibilities as core values of the school's community are central.

Conclusion

In this chapter, we explored the concepts and research behind SEL and CRSL. We learned about the impetus for this work in schools, how both practices can positively impact the school community and improve learning experiences for students, and the role of the transformational leader in creating a culture of care. Throughout the chapter, we've had the opportunity to reflect on our own school communities, our leadership, and the culture of care we are creating or seek to create.

In the next chapter, we will delve into bridging the gap between CRSL and SEL using the tenets of CRASEL. After engaging in the following reflective questions, please see the suggested "Potential Action Steps" reproducible (page 28) to help you implement these protocols in your school.

Questions for Reflection and Discussion

Please reflect on the following questions, alone or in a book discussion group, to consider the chapter content and your current and future leadership practices.

1. What new knowledge did you gain about CRSL and SEL?
2. Where did you find a connection to your leadership philosophy?
3. In what area do you feel a disconnect? What might be the reason for the disconnect, and what could you do to address it?
4. When considering your school community, where do you see opportunities to integrate or build on culturally responsive and SEL practices?
5. What strategies or practices shared in the chapter would you like to explore further? Why?

Potential Action Steps

In the potential action steps for chapter 1, you have the opportunity to deepen the work and operationalize a practice or practices you and your team would like to begin with. Choose as many or as few as you are able. Consider quality over quantity and think of these possible action steps as opportunities to grow, strengthen, and build on as opposed to steps to take all at once.

- Work with your school community and leadership team to identify the practices you currently use that reflect social-emotional learning (SEL) and a culturally responsive approach. Use a research-based common definition or framework for SEL and culturally responsive school leadership (CRSL). Various resources may be helpful, such as:
    - Gloria Ladson-Billings's (1995a, 1995b) framework for culturally relevant pedagogy
    - Zaretta Hammond's (2015) Ready for Rigor framework
    - CASEL framework (CASEL, n.d.)
    - Muhammad A. Khalifa, Mark Anthony Gooden, and James Earl Davis's (2016) culturally responsive leadership framework
    - Gholdy Muhammad's (2020) historical literacy framework
- Review your school's written mission and vision and determine whether they reflect SEL and CRSL according to the definitions or frameworks your community has chosen.
- Determine whether your school's current mission and vision reflect the school you want to be. If they do not, engage the school community through a town hall or series of surveys with various stakeholders and identify what more you need for your school to reach its ideal place in terms of SEL and CRSL. These survey questions can be similar to questions in an equity audit, such as:
    - In what ways is this school how you want it to be in terms of CRSL and SEL? (Be specific and name practices and policies.)
    - In what ways is it not reflective of CRSL and SEL? (Be specific and name practices and policies.)
    - What desired outcomes would you expect for students if CRSL and SEL were at the forefront?
    - What actions should you take to ensure that school practices and policies reflect CRSL and SEL?

- What actions should teachers and support staff take to ensure that classroom practices reflect CRSL and SEL?
- What supports and involvement do you need from families to ensure that CRSL and SEL become a part of the school's mission and vision?

Note: Remember, this work will take time. It is continuous and ongoing. Pace yourself according to the needs of your community.

References

CASEL. (n.d.). *What is the CASEL framework?* Accessed at https://casel.org/fundamentals-of-sel/what-is-the-casel-framework on March 18, 2024.

Hammond, Z. (2015). *Culturally responsive teaching and the brain: Promoting authentic engagement and rigor among culturally and linguistically diverse students.* Thousand Oaks, CA: Corwin.

Khalifa, M. A., Gooden, M. A., & Davis, J. E. (2016). Culturally responsive school leadership: A synthesis of the literature. *Review of Educational Research, 86*(4), 1272–1311. http://dx.doi.org/doi:10.3102/0034654316630383

Ladson-Billings, G. (1995a). But that's just good teaching! The case for culturally relevant pedagogy. *Theory Into Practice, 34*(3), 159–165.

Ladson-Billings, G. (1995b). Toward a theory of culturally relevant pedagogy. *American Educational Research Journal, 32*(3), 465–491. http://dx.doi.org/https://doi.org/10.3102%2F00028312032003465

Muhammad, G. (2020). *Cultivating genius: An equity framework for culturally and historically responsive literacy.* New York: Scholastic.

2

Practicing Culturally Responsive and Affirming Social-Emotional Leadership (CRASEL)

In the previous chapter, we discussed CRSL and SEL. This chapter outlines a bridge between the two practices. We refer to this bridge as *CRASEL*, which stands for *culturally responsive and affirming social-emotional leadership*. Once leaders build awareness and shift mindsets, they then need to shift to implementation that will impact students, staff, and families directly. To ensure students have a consistent experience, we detail the steps you can take to build a culture of care throughout the school community and enact the CRASEL framework. We will outline key definitions used in discussing these topics, as it is crucial to establish common understandings of these terms.

Dawn embarked on a qualitative composite case study of the beliefs, values, and care and leadership practices of urban principals in New York City in 2020. We will refer to this going forward as the Brooks DeCosta study. The Brooks DeCosta (2020) study resulted in the CRASEL framework. This framework combines the findings from the study with ideas from two other key frameworks: the CASEL framework for SEL (CASEL, n.d.), and Khalifa and colleagues' (2016) CRSL framework. The Brooks DeCosta (2020) study notes that "little research is available on the connections between SEL and culturally responsive approaches. . . . Although both seek to provide a positive learning environment for students in urban settings, they are seen in isolation from one another" (p. 55). We hope that the CRASEL framework addresses this disparity and proves a valuable resource for educators.

In this chapter, we also reflect on our own experiences with SEL and our perspectives on how students' crises manifest in their behavior. We explore school discipline policies to determine where we can be more culturally responsive as we support students socially and emotionally. We hear Mark's perspective as he works to support leaders and educators. We will also detail the CRASEL framework and the specific actions you can take in your leadership to combine these established practices of SEL and CRSL that enhance one another and your school learning environments.

Words From a Principal

SEL has become popular in the education world. When I started incorporating SEL practices as a teacher in the early 2010s, they were not widely heard of or valued. I recognized, however, once Craig Richards at Teachers College, Columbia University, introduced me to the practices, that the self-awareness work he engaged aspiring leaders in would be equally beneficial to students, teachers, and even families struggling with the daily stresses and challenges of life.

I also recognized that what I learned about SEL made me think of the caring educators I experienced as a student and as a colleague. I specifically remember an early childhood paraprofessional at a school where I worked early in my education career, Ms. R. She was a graceful, compassionate, older Black woman who loved her job supporting children. She was attentive to every detail, and I can picture her now—her perfectly curled hair, her smile, and a white lab coat she wore every day. Ms. R had a way of soothing, calming, and encouraging students who had the most challenging of behaviors to manage.

Being new to the profession and not having the classroom management skills I needed, I was in awe of the relationships she had not only with the students, but with the staff and parents as well. What I also remember, in this school with a 100 percent Black and Brown student population, was that she understood the underlying life circumstances, situations, and triggers that some of the students were experiencing. She knew the families, and she lived in the community. Her understanding allowed her to approach their emotional needs with love and without blame. Even during a crisis, she would speak to the student's best self and their potential. Students' behaviors and reactions didn't diminish her expectation for them. It did not matter how angry, how disrespectful, or how emotionally or even physically aggressive a student may have been; she would speak to their highest self. There was forgiveness and an unconditional love, no matter how many times it had happened before. And it directly impacted how the students felt about themselves and their behavior, giving them a self-concept and knowledge that they were loved that allowed them to persevere through the crisis.

Ms. R wasn't trained in SEL. Her words were simple; she didn't have a repertoire of vocabulary or SEL prompts, tips, or tools. I remember one student, Brian, who was in daily crisis. His life circumstances were difficult for a child as young as he was. He had a hard exterior, but we knew it was a coping mechanism he used to avoid being hurt or rejected. So, no matter how angry he tried to be, we showered him with love. Ms. R would say, even when Brian was scowling and working up to an outburst, "Look at the nice Brian—he is trying so hard. Look, isn't he wonderful?"

She would repeatedly draw attention to every positive thing he did or said, and Brian would regulate his emotions and strive to get more of that same positive attention. Even though Brian was in kindergarten at the time, we could see that he felt he had to always be "strong" as a survival technique. Ms. R held the same high expectations for Brian as for any other student. She saw him, the wholeness of who he was, including his life context and the impact it had on his emotions. We didn't know that was SEL at the time. But every time I had the benefit of being in her presence with the students, I experienced a master class in culturally responsive SEL. It was something I did not learn in my teacher development studies. I began to use the strategies I learned from Ms. R, and I still use them to this day in my leadership.

RELATE AND REFLECT
- Can you see how students like Brian might be labeled a problem? Can you think of students in your environment whose emotions are impacted by their upbringing or home context, and whose behaviors are misinterpreted?
- How might Brian's situation be potentially mishandled and worsened by someone who didn't see him in a holistic way, who didn't consider his underlying circumstances?
- How do you think Ms. R's encouragement and praise of Brian also affected his relationships with his peers?

Words From a Professor

In the winter of 2011, I visited Yale University to attend a workshop and obtain Mayer-Salovey-Caruso Emotional Intelligence Test (MSCEIT) training certification. The sessions included leaders from all over the United States but were small and led by David Caruso, one of the authors of the MSCEIT assessment, along with John Mayer and Peter Salovey. At the time, I was serving as director of the University of Texas at Austin Principalship Program, and I was looking for a way to support leaders in embracing the intense emotional work needed to become antiracist. The assistant *program director, Ann O'Doherty, accompanied me and received the training as well. While we thought it was useful, we noted that there was absolutely no engagement around race, racism, and culture. These social concepts were relevant, but unless the leader engaged with them directly, they were certain to be underprepared to address school inequities. Despite the usefulness of the training, we thought then—as I do now—that avoiding racism and culture was a serious shortcoming in the exciting work of emotional intelligence.*

While there, Ann and I learned that the history of emotional intelligence goes back to 1990, when Salovey and Mayer (1990b) cowrote a scholarly article on the subject. And then in 1995, Daniel Goleman authored what would become a popular book on emotional intelligence, and the field of SEL sprang from this effort. SEL nowadays refers to a process in which students acquire emotional intelligence, develop empathy for others, and learn problem-solving skills. However, what I recognized then and now is that SEL must incorporate an understanding of how race and racism are relevant to be most impactful and useful to leaders. In other words, our SEL work must understand the cultural context, just as Ms. R did, each and every day.

This is why we are proposing that leaders wishing to do any work related to SEL take time to develop critical consciousness, which involves "developing a deep understanding of systems of historical oppression, which enables school leaders to conceptualize how to create equity based on the current conditions and resources of their school" (Gooden et al., 2023, p. 4). For many leaders, especially those who have been minoritized, endeavoring to develop a deep understanding of historical systems of oppression is likely to evoke personal emotions of the leaders and/or the staff members. Additionally, critical consciousness helps leaders recognize what it means to care and to empathize with a Black or Brown student who might be living through some tough economic circumstances that are influenced by a sociocultural context. Leaders who aspire to be more culturally responsive cannot do so without undertaking a deep commitment to develop their critical consciousness. I would add that the CRASEL model, which we introduce in this chapter, suggests that they also consider how well they manage their emotions and support the emotions of others. In the next sections, we shed some light on how to bring CRSL and SEL together to support students.

Definitions of Key Terms

For the purposes of this chapter and work in schools, it is crucial that you use common definitions related to culturally responsive and relevant pedagogy and SEL. Here are the definitions we will use to describe both CRSL and SEL practices and the associated terms that connect the two.

- **Culturally relevant pedagogy:** Ladson-Billings (1995a) defines *culturally relevant pedagogy* as "a way of teaching students in which they (a) experience academic success; (b) develop and/or maintain cultural competence; and (c) develop a critical consciousness" (p. 160).

- **Culturally responsive pedagogy:** Gay's (2002) definition of *culturally responsive pedagogy* is "using the cultural characteristics, experiences, and perspectives of ethnically diverse students as conduits for teaching them more effectively" (p. 106).

- **Culturally responsive school leadership:** Grounded in the work of Ladson-Billings (1995a, 1995b) and Gay (1994, 2002, 2010), *culturally responsive school leadership (CRSL)* is leadership where the leader critically self reflects on leadership behaviors, develops culturally responsive teachers, promotes culturally responsive and inclusive school environments, and engages students, parents, and local contexts (Khalifa et al., 2016).

- **Culturally responsive sustaining education:** As defined by the New York State Education Department (2019), *culturally responsive sustaining education (CRSE)* is "intended to help education stakeholders create student-centered learning environments that affirm cultural identities; foster positive academic outcomes; develop students' abilities to connect across lines of difference; elevate historically marginalized voices; empower students as agents of social change; and contribute to individual student engagement, learning, growth, and achievement through the cultivation of critical thinking" (pp. 6–7).

- **Emotional intelligence:** Salovey and Mayer (1990a) coined the term *emotional intelligence (EI)*, describing it as "a form of social intelligence that involves the ability to monitor one's own and others' feelings and emotions, to discriminate among them, and to use this information to guide one's thinking and action" (p. 5).

- **Social-emotional learning:** Joseph E. Zins and Maurice J. Elias (2007) define *social-emotional learning (SEL)* as "the capacity to recognize and manage emotions, solve problems effectively, and establish positive relationships with others," which they argue are "competencies that clearly are essential for all students" (p. 1).

- **Whole-child education:** Velma LaPoint, Constance M. Ellison, and A. Wade Boykin (2006) define the education of the *whole child* as "an approach where there is a focus on the proactive, interactive and comprehensive cultivation of children's development within their natural developmental frame of reference as well as their historical and existing functional cultural context" (p. 374). In this book, we also use the term *holistic* in this context.

Using consistent terminology can dispel and combat misinformation and inaccuracies about enacting such policies.

A Culture of Care

A way to connect SEL and a culturally responsive approach is the creation of an authentic culture of caring. Creating a culture of care in a school community is multifaceted. It requires that administration and school staff are responsive to the holistic needs of all members of the school community. SEL alone is not sufficient to meet the holistic needs that include a student's cultural and social identity. As Brooks DeCosta notes (2020):

> In terms of teacher development, we as humans are cultural beings and, as such, hold our own perceptions and worldviews that impact our service to others. Teachers who also are in the service of others must acknowledge the individual cultural differences that may impact the treatment and perceptions of those whom they serve who may not share their cultural background. There must be an effort to learn and acknowledge the cultures of others to hold a more multicultural approach. (pp. 50–51)

Schools must adapt to address the individual needs of the students they serve and the world they are preparing them for. These needs include the following.

- Students' social and emotional needs
- Students' basic life needs that are within the purview of the school
- Students' needs that connect with their individual cultures and identities

Creating this holistically responsive school environment is foundational to the quality of the learning environment.

Both social-emotional supports and culturally responsive approaches enhance the learning experience for all students. They can learn in an environment that sees them as whole individuals, recognizes their needs, and acknowledges and incorporates who they are to connect students with the content they are learning. The sense of belonging and connection that is created through authentic caring builds the foundation of social and emotional trust. Part of building that trust includes educators and leaders connecting to and celebrating the diversity of culture and perspectives that students and their families bring to the learning environment based on their upbringing, identities, and experiences. It is crucial that educators see their students and their families from a place of caring that acknowledges their sociopolitical context and approaches their learning and care with that context in mind.

As mentioned in chapter 1 (page 9), the role of the transformational leader is key in enacting this approach. The risks leaders take in this work are great, especially in environments where cultural responsiveness in schools is inaccurately perceived as teaching groups of students to hate themselves or the history of the United States. Lisa Harrison, Ellis Hurd, and Kathleen Brinegar (2021) note from the perspective of middle school educators that the bans outlined in legislation passed in states such as Arizona, Idaho, Iowa, New Hampshire, Oklahoma, South Carolina, Tennessee, and Texas prohibit "teaching concepts, such as systemic racism, conscious or unconscious bias, and privilege" (pp. 2–3). In addition, they explain how the legislation also prohibits teaching practices that many teachers hold as ideal, such as teaching students to examine, explore, and question issues including race, racism, and discrimination.

Depending on laws being passed in certain states across the United States, leaders and teachers take extreme risks in teaching students about diversity and the history of race. Some states, however, such as New York, further commit and require systems and practices in schools that are equitable and center culturally responsive education and SEL. The following sections detail some ways that bridging SEL and CRSL can have unique benefits.

Approaches to Discipline

Teachers' preservice programming and coursework may not adequately prepare them to manage challenging student emotions, which causes them to struggle with classroom management and impacts the quality of student learning. When teachers come from universities and colleges that do not include and prioritize this work, the school leader must find and provide the ongoing professional development, coaching, mentoring, and support for new teachers to effectively implement SEL and CRSL without causing additional harm.

A way to connect social-emotional learning and a culturally responsive approach is the creation of an authentic culture of caring.

The U.S. Department of Education Office for Civil Rights (2014) finds that Black and Brown students are suspended and expelled at a greater rate than White students. Melanie Leung-Gagné, Jennifer McCombs, Caitlin Scott, and Daniel J. Losen (2022) state that in data collected across the United States, "educators consistently exclude Black students from school at the highest rate, with more than 1 in 8 Black students (12%) receiving one or more out-of-school suspensions in 2017–18" (p. 4). Christerralyn Brown, Daniel M. Maggin, and Molly Buren (2018) cite a study (Carrero, Collins, & Lusk, 2017) showing that "while one-third of students with emotional or behavioral disorders were students of color, three-fourths of students identified as at risk were minorities" (p. 433). In the same study, Brown and colleagues (2018) note specifically that "Black students comprised nearly 90% of students of color" (p. 433). Khalifa and colleagues (2016) write that "the discipline gap—which is often characterized by racialized disparities in disciplinary referrals, suspensions, expulsions, and court citations—is a direct indication that school cultures are hostile toward minoritized students" (p. 1279).

School leaders should be aware of the disparity in such suspensions as they relate to race and use a restorative approach to discipline. Students' inability to excel academically can result from an absence of a safe and nurturing classroom culture, which SEL provides. Students can exhibit attention-seeking behaviors through disruption or disengagement to mitigate the attention they are not receiving. Rectifying this will require that schools as early as preK begin providing multiple opportunities for students to feel supported, nurtured, and validated in their emotions and give them opportunities to practice the self-care methods that will positively impact their mental health and their interactions and relationships with others. Throughout schooling, in group work and through partnerships, we have ample opportunities to support students and nurture their development through learning to share, resolve conflicts, manage stress, and discuss and interact with others in classrooms.

Schools that use a zero-tolerance approach to discipline can further marginalize students of color. Punitive measures misaligned with the support students need can increase harm. Sue Winton (2013) emphasizes that "emotional supports for students at risk of academic failure and misbehavior, caring relationships, and developmentally appropriate interventions that focus on correction and learning from one's mistakes are alternatives to zero tolerance" (p. 468).

Students who lack a sense of belonging can instead disrupt classrooms and are often suspended or removed from the learning environment. Khalifa and colleagues (2016) note the long-lasting impact of suspension on a student's ability to succeed and maintain the needed positive relationships with teachers and peers. In classrooms that prioritize SEL, students feel connected and experience a sense of trust that allows them to recognize and regulate emotions that might otherwise result in maladaptive behaviors (Brooks DeCosta, 2020).

Lisa Delpit (2006), Karen M. Higgins and Jean Moule (2009), and H. Richard Milner (2006) suggest that high expectations are a central component of a culturally responsive approach. When educators believe in the potential of their students and hold high expectations for them, those students strive to meet those expectations. The SEL approach centered in CRSE prepares students for a life that is joyful and productive through support and consistent practice with the social-emotional skills they will need to have positive relationships with self, family, friends, and colleagues, and ultimately success in their endeavors.

In schools where the leaders and teachers feel a sense of connectedness to the students, as well as a true belief in their potential while holding high expectations for them, teachers restore, uplift, and heal students rather than use punitive measures for "correcting" behavior. In the CRASEL approach bridging SEL and CRSE, SEL is used not as a behavior control system but rather as a system for free expression, validation, and opportunities for supporting students' needs.

Approaches to Identity

Scholars Pamela W. Garner, Duhita Mahatmya, Elizabeth L. Brown, and Colleen K. Vesely (2014) indicate that "both cultural and social factors shape SEL" (p. 167) and furthermore the sociocultural capabilities of teachers and school leaders impact the delivery of the social-emotional program itself. Connecting with and attempting to understand the experiences, life situations, and cultural traditions of students are essential to be able to respond to their needs within context.

Michael Hughes, K. Jill Kiecolt, Verna M. Keith, and David H. Demo (2015) note that a positive self-concept and sense of identity are directly linked to student mental health and well-being. This is where CRSE and SEL overlap, teaching students the value and beauty of diversity and having them experience themselves in the learning, texts, and content in positive, organic ways. Learning about the contributions and achievements of diverse people gives students a positive sense of identity. *All* students, of all races and backgrounds, need to learn more about themselves and one another to create a sense of belonging and connectedness across cultures. The leaders and teachers at a school can facilitate this by creating experiences for students.

> *In the CRASEL approach bridging SEL and CRSE, SEL is used not as a behavior control system but rather a system for free expression, validation, and opportunities for supporting students' needs.*

Very plainly, the ways students see themselves and feel about themselves, and the ways they are made to see themselves and feel about themselves, are directly tied to their mental health and well-being. This is the foundation of CRASEL. This indicates why a *colorblind* approach that ignores student racial and cultural identity and experience is counterproductive toward the positive self-concept we want students to achieve. When we are colorblind, we erase and devalue an important aspect of our students' identities, as if it is something we wish not to see. Affirmations of diverse cultures are beneficial to students' identity development. Where populations lack diversity, sharing positive experiences with diverse cultural identities also supports the development of students' concept of their connections to other cultures and the world. In a whole-child approach, identity is something to be recognized, affirmed, and celebrated.

Approaches to Culture

Another key aspect of CRASEL bridging CRSE and SEL is recognizing and acknowledging how students' diverse life experiences and cultural norms impact their emotional state and expression. In addition to colorblindness, there are other barriers to SEL practices that lack a culturally responsive approach. Researchers Dena N. Simmons, Marc A. Brackett, and Nancy Adler (2018) find that "five barriers contribute to inequitable access to a high-quality SEL education" (p. 2), specifically, "poverty, exclusionary discipline [practices and policies], lack of trauma-informed practices, implicit bias [in school staff], and educator stress and burnout" (p. 6). Simmons and colleagues (2018) propose the following strategies to mitigate those barriers.

- School racial and socioeconomic integration initiatives
- Restorative justice practices for school discipline
- Trauma-informed system interventions
- Culturally competent and equity-literate educators
- SEL and mindfulness programming to support students and teachers (p. 2)

As mentioned earlier, Black and Brown students are impacted socially, emotionally, and physiologically by racism at increased instances as compared to White students, and their emotional well-being is compromised (Brooks DeCosta, 2020). Michelle G. Knight-Manuel and Joanne E. Marciano (2019) assert that "enacting culturally relevant teaching and learning practices throughout a school environment can provide more-equitable opportunities to ensure that all students, particularly culturally and linguistically diverse students, are supported academically, socially, emotionally, and civically in an increasingly diverse global society" (as cited in Brooks DeCosta, 2020, p. 53).

Transformative leadership that values social justice is vital to ensuring groups of students are not further marginalized. The success of schoolwide policies and practices begins with the emphasis from a culturally responsive school leader who prioritizes this work.

Words From a Principal

At TMALS, we prioritize the integration of SEL with CRSE. Our beloved third-grade teacher, Ms. Turner, created a lesson that serves as a clear example of the integration of CRSE and SEL. She engages students in an "affirmation station," where students walk in every morning and look in a mirror that she has on her door with affirmations around it. Students say an affirmation aloud such as "I am worthy," "I am significant," "I am unique," "I am intelligent," and so on.

Ms. Turner designed a lesson focused on the art of Bisa Butler, which uses historical images to highlight the beauty of Black people using a quilt medium. Education scholar Gholdy Muhammad collaborated with Butler to create guiding essential questions for the study of the work. After learning about the inspiration and reflecting on Butler's work, Ms. Turner had students read the text I Like Myself! *by Karen Beaumont (2004). Her students then wrote "I Am" poems. While they worked, they listened to Beyoncé's (2019) "Brown Skin Girl," a song whose lyrics they examined as well.*

This culturally responsive lesson addresses and combats deficit stereotypical images of Blackness through an examination of work that lifts the beauty of Black people. It centered the humanity of Black people, a concept beneficial to all races of students. At the same time, students were able to connect to their own beauty, increasing their positive self-concept. Muhammad's books Cultivating Genius *(2020) and* Unearthing Joy *(2023) share various culturally responsive lesson plans and ideas for educators to adapt.*

CRASEL Origins

Schools that attend to the cultural, social, and emotional needs of their school community members exhibit a culture of care. This holistic approach creates a flourishing community where students, staff, and families have strong positive relationships, feel diversity is affirmed, and feel a sense of belonging and connectedness. As we mentioned in the chapter introduction, the Brooks DeCosta study is a qualitative composite case study of the beliefs, values, and care and leadership practices of urban principals in New York City in 2020. Brooks DeCosta

(2020) finds three key themes in her exploration of school leaders' perspectives and their practices of caring: caring for students, caring for the community, and leaders caring for themselves. Her study concludes with "implications for practice and a proposed framework that bridges social-emotional learning and culturally relevant and responsive approaches to urban school leadership" (p. iii). The CRASEL framework is a result of that study.

Figure 2.1 represents how school leaders in the study center and prioritize their own self-care, the care of their students, and the care of the school community. Surrounding the members of the school community are the social-emotional practices the school employs, which are encased in the positive relationships between the members of the community in caring for one another. The umbrella around the culture of care is the overall culturally responsive approach.

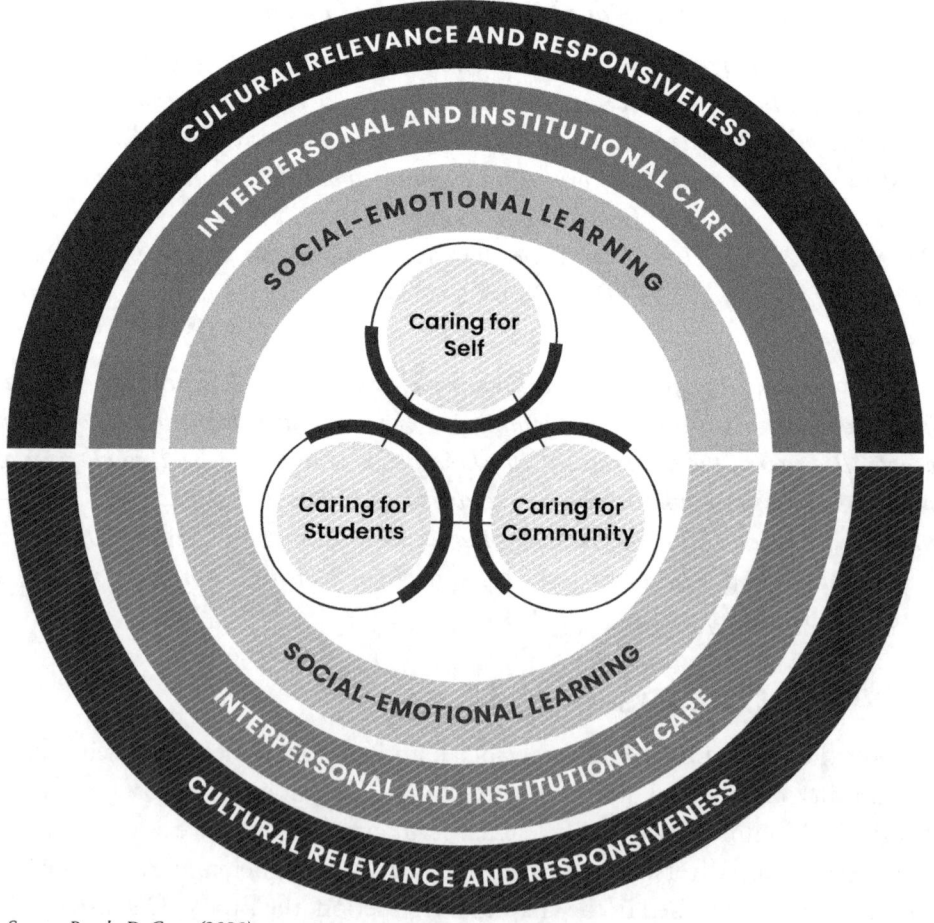

Source: Brooks DeCosta (2020).
Figure 2.1: Themes of school leaders' perspectives and their practices of caring.

In the following sections, we look in detail at the three major components of a culture of care: caring for students, caring for community, and caring for self.

Caring for Students

The principals Brooks DeCosta (2020) interviewed felt it was necessary to help their students, teachers, and families find a sense of calm, and each relied on practices and routines that prepared them for their workdays. Principals exercised routines of care for students that included the following.

- Knowing students well, including their sociocultural, sociopolitical, and socioeconomic needs and experiences
- Engaging staff in professional development on strength- or asset-based mindsets
- Providing opportunities for implicit bias workshops
- Providing targeted academic supports for students
- Engaging staff in professional learning community book studies using professional texts on CRSL and SEL
- Interrupting deficit mindsets about students and families as they surface
- Engaging in self-reflection regarding language and actions
- Engaging the community in creating a vision for racial equity
- Training staff and utilizing restorative circles as a positive approach to discipline and conflict
- Engaging staff in an audit of policies and practices that marginalize students (Brooks DeCosta, 2020)

The care of students includes caring for the staff who support them daily. Supporting the adults who are in direct contact with students is imperative. While creating a culture where students' identities are validated and they feel seen and supported in ways that allow them to thrive academically, staff must be supported in creating this atmosphere in their classrooms. Professional development for staff that includes self-reflection, development in an equity-based approach, strategies for restorative practice, and a growth mindset will directly impact students.

Caring for Community

In their seminal work *Race-ing Moral Formation*, Vanessa Siddle Walker and John R. Snarey (2004) note that "care means liberating others from their state of need and actively promoting their welfare" (p. 4). Examples provided by leaders in the Brooks DeCosta (2020) study of caring for their communities include the following.

- Hosting family engagement events
- Knowing families well, including their sociocultural, sociopolitical, and socioeconomic needs and experiences
- Communicating with families often and staying connected regularly
- Viewing families as a resource of cultural knowledge
- Including families in decision making within the school community
- Soliciting family collaboration with school staff to co-create the school's mission, vision, and focus
- Gauging family interest in workshops and events
- Supporting family needs (food, jobs, training, resources) outside of the school community
- Engaging families as active participants in the school community
- Serving as a vocal advocate in outer community needs and concerns (Walker & Snarey, 2004)

Leaders who care for families include them in the school community. Families are a valued part of the care of students. This can happen collaboratively when families are given agency and are empowered to experience the school's mission and vision in tangible ways. When schools treat families as merely receivers of information and not as active participants, they are missing an impactful lever in the success of the students.

Caring for Self

The leaders Brooks DeCosta (2020) interviewed shared the following self-care strategies they engage in regularly.

- Physical exercise
- Conversations with friends and family at the end of the day
- Prayer or meditation before and during the day
- Outings with loved ones
- Listening to music
- Aromatherapy or spa visits
- Mindful eating
- Health and wellness commitments
- Positive affirmations and intentions at the start of the day

- Vision boards
- Mentorship or coaching

This approach to creating a culture of care is multifaceted and focuses on the direct care of the individual. Among school leaders, there is a tendency to prioritize the care of others. While this is important, for sustainability and effectiveness, the leader must also prioritize their own self-care and mental and physical health.

The CRASEL Framework

The CRASEL framework, as shown in figure 2.2, encompasses the competencies and practices of a culturally responsive and affirming social-emotional leader and the actions they must take, starting with self-reflection and self-awareness. This work is continual and ongoing, hence the figure's cyclical design. Depending on the school community's needs, leaders may choose to emphasize some areas more than others and adjust the sequence.

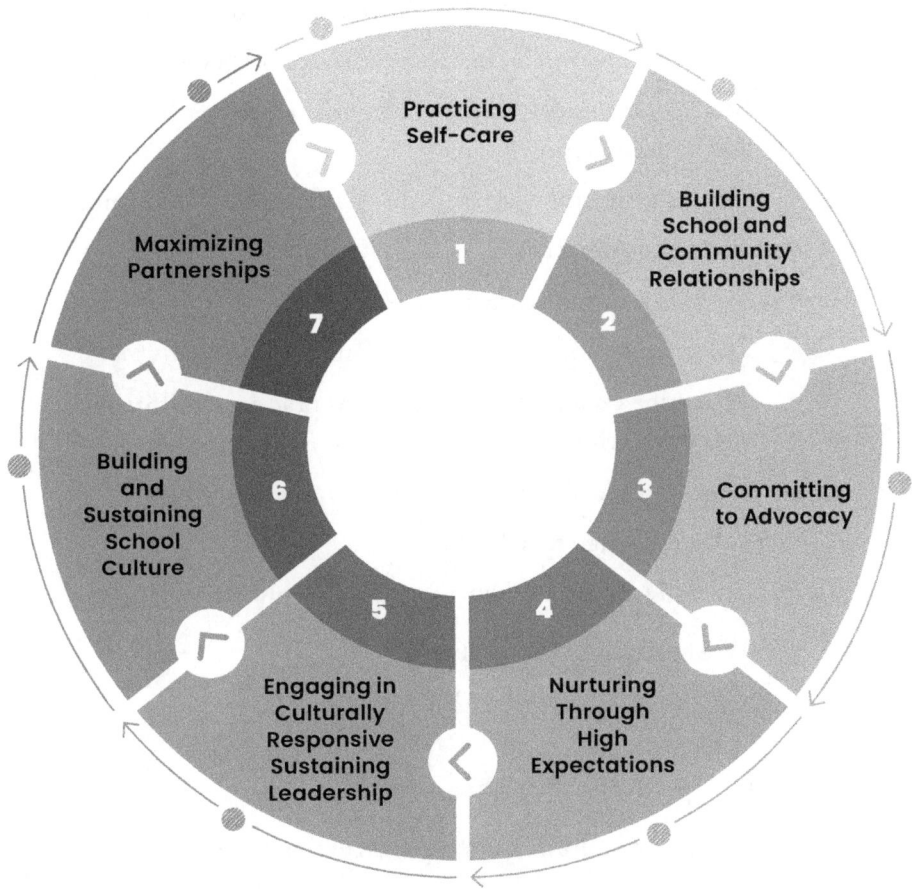

Source: Brooks DeCosta (2020).
Figure 2.2: The culturally responsive and affirming social-emotional leadership (CRASEL) framework.

The following list details specific elements of the CRASEL framework shown in figure 2.2 (page 45).

1. **Practicing Self-Care**
    - Recognize and identify emotions and the impact on the school community
    - Self-reflect on leadership behaviors and actions
    - Manage stress
    - Practice mindfulness
    - Engage in self-motivation
    - Practice self-regulation, self-awareness, and self-management
    - Compose a racial autobiography

2. **Building School and Community Relationships**
    - Maintain supportive, understanding, and positive communication with all staff, students, and families
    - Hone ability to take the perspectives of others with empathy
    - Be a servant leader; find connections between school and community
    - Connect directly with students, staff, families, and community

3. **Committing to Advocacy**
    - Serve as a caring advocate
    - Resist deficit images of students and families
    - Challenge exclusionary policies and practices within and outside of school
    - Serve as a social activist for school and community
    - Value students' social capital
    - Cultivate an asset-based approach schoolwide

4. **Nurturing Through High Expectations**
    - Create a safe environment for all learners
    - Engage student voice
    - Practice positive discipline
    - Use data to inform students' instructional needs

- Ensure an academic program that is rigorous and challenging for diverse learners
- Curate and provide high-quality professional development
- Create a culture of intervisitation and peer feedback
- Create lab classrooms

5. **Engaging in Culturally Responsive Sustaining Leadership**
    - Develop a culturally responsive staff
    - Use data to determine student needs and areas of unfinished learning
    - Model culturally responsive practices throughout the school day and in all spaces of the school
    - Incorporate identity and perspectives of the marginalized into the curriculum
    - Conduct an equity audit
    - Develop a vision for racial equity

6. **Building and Sustaining School Culture**
    - Co-create the vision
    - Articulate tangible aspects
    - Align practices, rituals, and routines
    - Model, uplift, and monitor professional learning communities
    - Curate and cultivate distributive leadership
    - Seek feedback regularly
    - Exhibit transparency and vulnerability

7. **Maximizing Partnerships**
    - Select high-quality partnerships
    - Connect partners to the mission and vision
    - Display commitment
    - Celebrate and share best practices widely
    - Connect partners to families
    - Give teachers opportunities to share their ideas and lead partner collaborations

Brooks DeCosta's (2020) proposed CRASEL framework:

> centers the school leaders' self-awareness, self-care, and self-management practices and the leadership practices that surround the school leader and their ability to sustain themselves. . . . The commitment to culturally responsive leadership; the beliefs and values that inform their nurturing for students and families; high expectations for themselves and the school community; the emphasis on community and relationship building; and the focus on advocacy and care for students, staff, and families are all central to the framework. These elements are cyclical and occur within and outside of one another. . . without care for the caregiver, the leader cannot sustain the work. (p. 134)

The chapters that follow highlight elements of the CRASEL framework and provide strategies for implementing it in your schools.

Conclusion

In this chapter, we discussed the need to ground SEL in a culturally responsive approach centering students' needs and their life experiences and contexts. CRSL and SEL must also inform the school discipline practices. You, as school leader, are significant as the lead learner in both SEL and culturally responsive approaches. We also presented the CRASEL framework and outlined the components that overlap and combine to create an approach that grounds all practices.

This work takes risk, consistency, vulnerability, research, collaboration, and motivation. Community leaders, politicians, educators, parents, and students must be courageous in prioritizing what they need in school as we combat racism and move toward a more just, compassionate, empathetic, and equitable society for all.

In chapter 3 (page 53), we will explore the need for leaders in demanding, high-accountability settings to engage in their own self-care practices. Preserving their own social, emotional, and physical health and well-being is necessary to create the sort of change we want to see in our schools. After engaging in the following reflective questions, please see the suggested "Potential Action Steps" reproducible (page 50) to help you implement these protocols in your school.

Questions for Reflection and Discussion

Please reflect on the following questions, alone or in a book discussion group, to consider the chapter content and your current and future leadership practices.

1. What new knowledge did you gain regarding CRASEL?
2. Where did you find a connection to CRASEL in your leadership philosophy?
3. In what area do you feel a disconnect? What might be the reason for the disconnect, and how might you address it?
4. In what ways can you serve as lead learner and model of CRASEL in your school community?

Potential Action Steps

In the potential action steps for chapter 2, you have the opportunity to deepen the work and operationalize a practice or practices you and your team would like to begin with. Choose as many or as few as you are able. Consider quality over quantity and think of these possible action steps as opportunities to grow, strengthen, and build on as opposed to steps to take all at once.

- Collaborate on and solidify the common definitions, terms, and frameworks that you and your school community will use for SEL and CRSL. Share those definitions, terms, and frameworks widely throughout the school community by providing them during professional development sessions, posting them visibly in the school, and sharing them with parent leadership teams.

- Once you spend ample time building the staff's knowledge base (and your own) in these practices, use the framework you've chosen to clearly define with your school community your reimagined mission and vision. Also determine what school data will show what CRSL and SEL will look like in your school in every classroom, office, and space of the school. Probing questions you can use to design your vision include the following.

    - Who do you want to be as a school community?
    - What is your desired outcome for students?
    - What routines, rituals, daily schedule components, curriculum and lesson structures, images, learning environments, and so on will be evident across classrooms and throughout the school?

- Seek input from all stakeholders in the community using your school's chosen combination of frameworks to create a checklist of non-negotiables for CRSL and SEL to add to your school's expectations and things to look for in instructional practice. School teams should co-create a checklist or walkthrough tool tailored to the school's needs and community. Possible examples might include the following.

    - Culturally diverse images throughout the classroom and school
    - Culturally responsive texts in classroom libraries
    - Visible strategies for emotional regulation
    - Restorative circles

- Calming corners
- Mindful practice as part of the daily schedule
- Curriculum that reflects diverse identities and perspectives

- Once you've completed the checklist, have all staff use it to conduct a self-assessment of their own classrooms to make needed adjustments in their instructional practices, routines, and environments.

- Appoint a model teacher for SEL practices and a model teacher for CRSE practices who will serve as lab instructors for intervisitations for staff who need development and for new staff. Consider teachers who excel and are passionate as well as those who have clear evidence of successful student work and outcomes in these areas.

- During faculty conferences or grade team meetings, conduct research-based article studies using the work of scholars in the CRSL and SEL fields to begin increasing the knowledge and content base for your staff in both areas. Suggested authors include Marc Brackett, James P. Comer, Sonya Douglass, Geneva Gay, Mark A. Gooden, Zaretta Hammond, Gloria Ladson-Billings, Linda Lantieri, Kofi Lomotey, Gholdy Muhammad, Django Paris, Dena Simmons, Robin Stern, and Linda Tillman. Use an article study protocol such as Harvard's Teaching and Learning Lab Discussion Protocols or the School Reform Initiative's 4A Text Protocol.

Note: Remember, this work will take time. It is continuous and ongoing. Pace yourself according to the needs of your community.

3

Prioritizing Self-Care

In this chapter, we will explore the concept of self-care, as well as self-awareness and self-management, as crucial to culturally responsive and affirming social-emotional leadership. These competencies are the first step of the CRASEL framework. With educators and leaders increasingly experiencing mental health crises because of the stresses of life, societal concerns, political unrest, and frustration with the education climate and demands, the need for these competencies has become more important as a survival mechanism for school leaders.

Words From a Principal

In the leadership academy I attended at Teachers College, Columbia University, Craig Richards, the director of and professor in the program, prioritized self-care. Unique to this program was a daily morning class focused on self-awareness and mindful practice. I had not heard of these practices before and, along with my classmates, was unsure why mindfulness and self-awareness were the focus of a course in a principals' preparation program. I will admit that in the beginning, it felt like a waste of time. For some of my classmates and me, it was difficult to tune everything out and engage in this unfamiliar practice. I was very accustomed to a fast, demanding pace as an educator, and this practice slowed life down considerably.

The first few days, there were giggles and lots of discomfort for most of us engaging in guided meditation, visualization, and reflective silence. At times I felt self-conscious and as if I didn't have a right to sit in silence this way. As the weeks went on, it became something I looked forward to. The sense of calm and centeredness afterward cleared my mind and allowed me a sense of lucidity and focus. These moments of created peace and quieting my mind were the only time and place I experienced that level of self-attention.

There was also an accountability structure within this practice through journaling. We journaled our feelings and experiences during the self-awareness class and submitted our journals weekly. I began to see the potential benefit of incorporating this practice in the elementary school classes I was teaching. I hoped the effect of calm and focus I experienced would be the same for my students. It was important to set an expectation and share the purpose with the students. I explained to them that this was a way to quiet the mind, which would allow them to focus more on their work and could improve their physical health. I began implementing it by playing quiet music while students were working and having five minutes of guided meditation at the beginning of each class. The students were young, grades K–5, but they engaged at their own developmentally appropriate levels.

As with my college classmates, my students had an adjustment period with giggles and discomfort. But after some consistency, they came to appreciate the opportunity to rest their minds without expectation. After years of incorporating this as a teacher, when I transitioned to leader, I was able to widen the implementation of these practices to all students in the school, and later to teachers, parents, and grandparents as well. Every morning, I led the entire school in a guided self-awareness meditation practice. Teachers appreciated the new calmness of the students at the start of class and the way the students started the day with a sense of peace and focus that impacted the rest of the day. As we did in my college course, many students came to expect and look forward to the mindful time together.

However, what was missing as I was engaging the school community in this practice each morning was a self-awareness and self-care practice for myself. The pace of being a new principal, the emotional and physical demands, the never-ending hours, and the lack of sleep began to take a toll on me physically. Out of nowhere, I developed a sense of anxiety and found my heart palpitating, eyes twitching, and hands shaking in times of stress. I had not experienced this before. I developed dark circles under my eyes and began to lose weight without explanation. The stress was clearly affecting my mental and physical health.

To combat the feelings of anxiety that began to feel like panic attacks, I started to use some of the breathing techniques I learned in the self-awareness class. Strategies like deep belly breathing became useful for me, and after some time, the anxiety, hand shaking, and palpitations disappeared. I realized why Dr. Richards prioritized this work as part of a principals' preparation program. He understood the toll the job would take on us, and he was providing a gift that would help us to survive. The ability to engage in self-awareness practice was a gift and a tool for wellness that I wanted to share with my school community to help with the everyday stresses we were all experiencing.

Words From a Professor

Concepts of self-care, self-awareness, and self-management are not usually found within the content of courses in leadership preparation programs. In fact, leaders have been taught implicitly or explicitly that to be successful, they must expect to be extremely busy meeting accountability goals and other incessant demands, all while being overextended in the role of building leaders. That approach emphasizes doing the job over taking care of themselves in the process. Commonly, school leaders are quick to remind others that they are frequently so busy each day that they often eat lunch three or four hours beyond the lunch hour, if they do at all. Additionally, the job is full of long days that are taxing emotionally and physically.

Few people besides other principals will truly understand how these stressors are experienced in the body and spirit. Even upon this realization, principal colleagues may decline to admit to themselves that this unchecked stress can be harmful. However, school leaders facing this kind of pressure will be hesitant to suggest that it is important to take time for themselves to reflect and rest, to take care of themselves, and to creatively engage the work of others in the tasks of the principalship. Relatedly, leaders need to be aware of emotions and able to manage them in ways that require them to ask for help when they need it.

While SEL leans toward managing the self, we would argue that combining it with CRSL pushes leaders not only to start with self-care but also to create an inclusive school environment and lean into culturally responsive instructional leadership. Inclusive school environments call on leaders to cultivate "spaces. . . welcoming to all, which requires a commitment to collaborating with individuals facing historical and existing barriers to inclusion to together reimagine and create a more culturally affirming context" (Gooden et al., 2023, p. 2).

Though the principal should lead this charge, doing so should not look like they are solely in charge of everything and everybody. Instead, an inclusive approach creates spaces and opportunities to develop others in the process of leading. This is especially impactful when leaders include staff who have been marginalized and are often not expected to contribute. To do this effectively, leaders will wisely seek to collaborate with colleagues who can assist them in realizing their vision to make the entire school more equitable. Engaging others in equity-focused leadership tasks like designing, discussing, and completing an equity audit can be extremely helpful in bringing along key members of the staff. Additionally, the principal should recruit leaders who can learn to address some of the major responsibilities of running the school. Though the principal will recruit staff to take on these exciting roles, they will still maintain responsibility for the whole operation. As a leader who enlists others, however, they will find more opportunities to support their overall emotional health.

While leaders are clearly important, there is research that reminds us that teachers still account for a larger percentage of classroom impact (Leithwood, 2014) and a larger percentage of student outcomes. Of course, these are limited ways of considering teacher and leader impact, as teachers are in partnership with leaders as they carefully consider the learning of students. Leaders must support teachers in reimagining existing pedagogy and curricula so that both honor knowledge associated with people of color, including their contributions and ways of engaging. Doing this challenges systems that exacerbate inequities by ignoring, misrepresenting, or rendering different approaches as marginal.

For too long, the contributions and experiences of Black and Brown people have been marginalized in America, if addressed or included at all. Having conversations with teachers who engage with the works of scholars such as those whose work we recommended in the "Potential Action Steps" reproducible in chapter 2 (page 50) can be affirming for students. While this might feel out of place when one considers the principal's emotional health, it is absolutely connected to the leader becoming more self-aware as this process becomes shared leadership. Additionally, there are teachers who can help lead the principal's charge of supporting the development of equity leadership teams (Radd, Generett, Gooden, & Theoharis, 2021).

RELATE AND REFLECT

- Can you relate to the experiences Dawn had with her physical and mental health because of work-related stress? How so?
- Do you see a need to incorporate self-care practices in your own leadership? What might that look like for you?
- What might prevent you from being consistent with your daily self-awareness or self-care practices?

Self-Care, Self-Awareness, and Self-Management

The CASEL framework for SEL defines *self-awareness* as "the ability to understand one's own emotions, thoughts, and values and how they influence behavior across contexts. This includes capacities to recognize one's strengths and limitations with a well-grounded sense of confidence and purpose" (CASEL, n.d.). CASEL further defines *self-management* as "the abilities to manage one's emotions, thoughts, and behaviors effectively in different situations and to achieve goals and aspirations. This includes the capacities to delay gratification, manage stress, and feel motivation and agency to accomplish personal and collective goals" (CASEL, n.d.). Both self-awareness and self-management are intrinsic to self-care.

In school leadership, it is essential to understand the emotions you experience as you manage the day-to-day stresses and high levels of accountability. Once you understand your own emotions and your personal reactions to events and people, you can use strategies to self-regulate. When we neglect to identify our emotions in a high-stress, high-variability position, we risk responding in ways that can negatively impact our leadership and the school community. Our staff, students, and families look to us for guidance. You, whether you want to or not, set a standard for behavior in your school community. All eyes are on you, watching and analyzing how you respond to stressful moments.

At the same time, this level of scrutiny can also serve as an opportunity to model the behaviors you want to see in your community. This requires that you hold a high level of emotional intelligence and self-awareness that allows you to identify your own triggers, be transparent with your limitations, and lean on your strengths in difficult situations. The variety of emotions we experience and must manage in a day, whether our own or in those we lead, can take a toll on us. Once we identify our strengths and limitations, we can then engage in our self-regulation strategies so we can respond to any given situation objectively and with a wider perspective beyond ourselves. Keeping the collective goal in mind and being strategic in our reactions directly impacts the outcome of current and future events.

Leading is relational, dispositional, and situational (Mutch, 2015). Leaders serve multiple groups of stakeholders, such as staff, students, families, caregivers, district offices, community, and political groups. Part of an effective leader's responsibility is building a collective purpose in the school community toward a common goal. Depending on the specific situation and the context of the school, you may need to operate as a changemaker. Change is difficult for people, and they may have an emotional reaction that can surface as resistance. Your capacity to connect with others, serve as an active listener, and regulate the emotions of others requires that you can regulate your own emotional response in service of the ultimate goal. You must use self-awareness to determine how much emotion to display and where it may be appropriate, as well as how much restraint to display if showing a certain type of emotion will negatively impact a situation or person.

Leadership capacities such as self-awareness and self-management are needed for facilitating teacher teams, making decisions, managing stressful situations, impacting improved classroom instruction, and seeing the perspectives of stakeholders with compassion (Gómez-Leal, Holzer, Bradley, Fernández-Berrocal, & Patti, 2022). Leaders are responsible and accountable for the decisions they make on behalf of the school community. These decisions directly impact the lives and experiences of others. The responsibility is great. In a school climate that is increasingly unpredictable, leaders must also manage situations that impact safety and the mental and physical health of the community. Marc Brackett (2019) describes this heavy lift for leaders as "emotional labour" (p. 129).

Leaders, in collaboration with organizations and policies, need to create safe, stable spaces for restoration and healing for their community in response to crisis (Dückers, Yzermans, Jong, & Boin, 2017). Trust building is also key and will come up as an important culture to build in this work. The ability to build trust is connected to one's own level of self-awareness and self-management. We will discuss the need to build trust in chapter 5 (page 83). Once leaders engage in the necessary self-reflection and self-awareness building, they are aware of their identities, perspectives, beliefs, motivations, and triggers, as well as the impact of their emotions and actions on others. Understanding the impact they have on others, leaders can manage those emotions and actions in ways that benefit their overall goals. In the midst of protecting the emotions of others, being a school leader can be a lonely job. Principals are caregivers, managers, problem solvers, fixers, accountability holders, and more. These roles can become stressful, heavy, and without relief, affecting the mental and physical health and wellness of the leader. Prioritizing, modeling, and creating opportunities for self-awareness and self-management as a leader is imperative if we are to function effectively and at our highest capacity while encouraging our staff and students to do the same.

The Importance of Self-Care

The pandemic and climate of school violence have required a new look at *crisis leadership*, where leaders must respond to disastrous events (Urick, Carpenter, &

Eckert, 2021). Unexpected events occur in school on any given day that require in-the-moment responses from school leaders. Emergency crises have created a new level of seriousness in day-to-day occurrences in schools. This has led to a need to focus on the burnout-level chronic stress many school leaders experience.

Principals are now leaving the profession due to burnout and excessive stress (Yan, 2020). In their work for the National Center for Education Statistics (NCES), Rebecca Goldring, Soheyla Taie, and Isaiah O'Rear (2018) note that principal turnover is at 18 percent across the United States. The demands of school leaders to hold responsibility for the physical and mental well-being of the school community and the accountability attached to that responsibility lead many into an unsustainable state of what Joshua Ray, John C. Pijanowski, and Kara Lasater (2020) refer to as "self-sacrifice" (p. 435). This can take the form of long hours, lack of sleep, neglecting to eat, missed doctor's appointments, taking work home, working on vacation days and weekends, and neglecting self-care, family, friends, and loved ones. This vicious cycle of self-neglect can negatively impact health, as Dawn described in her experiences as a new principal.

> *The ability to build trust is connected to one's own level of self-awareness and self-management.*

Prioritizing self-care, although not widely studied, can mitigate principal stress and help to avoid burnout. The National Institute of Mental Health (n.d.) defines *self-care* as "taking the time to do things that help you live well and improve both your physical health and mental health." Lisa D. Butler, Kelly A. Mercer, Katie McClain-Meeder, Dana M. Horne, and Melissa Dudley (2019) identify two goals of self-care: (1) to "guard against, cope with, or reduce stress and related adverse experiences" and (2) to "maintain or enhance well-being and overall functioning" (pp. 107–108). Butler and colleagues (2019) continue by outlining six aspects of self-care that professionals must be mindful of to prevent chronic stress, psychological stress-related trauma, and burnout. Butler and colleagues' (2019) six self-care areas are as follows.

1. **Physical:** Care of the physical body
2. **Professional:** Reducing work-related risks
3. **Relational:** Nourishing interpersonal relationships
4. **Emotional:** Mitigating negative emotional experiences and creating positive emotional experiences

5. **Psychological:** Attending to intellectual needs
6. **Spiritual:** Reflection on the inner self and relationship to the universe. (p. 109)

To retain principals and increase their efficacy, those who supervise them can provide support by prioritizing principal health and wellness. As the principal sets the tone for the school, "healthy principals that prioritize their well-being can sustain efforts to improve schools, and support teachers, interrogate inequitable policies and practices that marginalize students, and build trusting relationships with families" (DeMatthews, Carrola, Reyes, & Knight, 2021, p. 165). If districts are unable or unwilling to provide their principals this support, then principals themselves need to develop self-care practices to meet their needs for physical, emotional, and mental well-being.

> Leaders must intentionally create a system and structure for themselves to prioritize self-care.

How to Establish a Self-Care Practice

With the pace of leadership, long hours, emotional drain, stress, and high accountability, it can be challenging to find the time or energy to practice self-care. Leaders must intentionally create a system and structure for themselves to prioritize self-care.

The following are recommendations for self-care practices for principals and other school leaders. You can adapt these to suit your needs and abilities.

- Delegate tasks on identified days so you can leave on time and avoid overtime hours on consecutive days during the week.
- Cultivate a personal or professional network that supports collective opportunities for self-care events and collaborative accountability (DeMatthews et al., 2021).
- Create opportunities to connect or debrief with mentors or peers when navigating challenging situations.
- Avoid skipping meals and prioritize having a task-free lunch whenever possible so you can focus on enjoying your meal.
- If possible, schedule times of day where you intentionally take walks around the school, allowing yourself time to periodically step away from emails and tasks involving the computer.

- Close your door to find solitude for a few minutes and develop a mindful practice that can involve calming music, deep breathing, or moments of silence to decompress and recenter yourself during times of stress or prior to handling a difficult conversation or situation.
- Avoid stress eating and incorporate a walking or exercise routine to decompress.
- Avoid taking work home and prioritize activities that you enjoy after work, on weekends, and on days off, such as time with family, outings with friends, yoga, visits to the spa, and so on.
- Listen to your body. Schedule and keep doctor's appointments and checkups on a regular basis.
- Prioritize eight hours of sleep each night.
- Drink water throughout the day to avoid dehydration.

The following recommendations indicate how district leaders can advocate for self-care practices in their districts. Again, you can adapt these to suit your needs and abilities.

- Create opportunities to check in with school leaders on their wellness and provide strategies and resources for those in need.
- Provide moments of self-care by incorporating time during supervisory meetings for reflection and emotional check-ins.
- Modify compliance expectations and demands of principals by pacing due dates in a way that avoids work overload and undue stress.
- Incorporate celebrations of success within supervisory meetings to increase optimism and motivation (DeMatthews et al., 2021).

The reproducible "Self-Care Reflection" tool at the end of the chapter (page 64) can help you reflect on your current practices regarding self-care and then brainstorm ways you can improve in these practices.

Words From a Principal

At TMALS, we invite everyone in the school community to engage in self-care practices. Through intentionally created mindful moments, students and staff engage in guided meditation every day, led by the teacher or a student leader. One of the common meditations we use is the loving-kindness meditation (Hutcherson, Seppala, & Gross, 2008). Teachers select the time of day these practices are needed most, either in times of stress, as a transition to a new subject matter, or after moments of high energy or excitement.

Through our work with the Pure Edge organization (see page 23), which has a free curriculum online, teachers, student leaders, and parents received training in mindful brain breaks, allowing them to help students recenter themselves, calm, and refocus. The brain responds to these activities by transferring focus to resting pathways in the brain that allow students to return to a state of focus, positive mood, and increased attention (Willis, 2016). Through the daily RULER Mood Meter check-ins (figure 1.1, page 25), participants can exercise self-awareness by reflecting, identifying, and recognizing their current emotional and physical state, naming the feeling, and then considering how they might regulate, if needed. In terms of creating a culture of self-care, the class community is also able to acknowledge the emotions of others and determine ways they can support one another. Mood Meter check-ins happen for staff during every faculty meeting, for parents through the ClassDojo online communications, and in interactive spaces throughout the school and schoolyard where large Mood Meters are available for anyone to utilize as a place to check in with themselves. We also have calming corners, which are beautiful spaces in the school building where anyone who needs a moment to decompress can sit and engage with the Mood Meter or chart of affirmations to help them self-manage and regulate any negative emotions impacting their day.

Student leaders are also trained as peer mediators, utilizing a RULER tool called the Blueprint to help manage conflict through self-awareness, self-reflection, self-management, and engaging the perspective and feelings of others. Similarly, teachers engage students in schoolwide weekly classroom restorative healing circles to help resolve classroom conflict and build relationships. Our guidance counselor, social worker, and administration also use the tools of the Blueprint and restorative practice in resolving larger ongoing conflicts that may include family members as well as students. Through the online platform Multitasking Yogi, students have weekly sessions with a certified yoga teacher who visits classrooms throughout the day, involving them in fifteen-minute yoga wellness push-ins to support their physical well-being.

TMALS makes use of mindfulness-based SEL practices that foster students' capacity to focus on learning with curiosity and nonjudgment (Bakosh, Snow, Tobias, Houlihan, & Barbosa-Leiker, 2015). Harlem Grown, an organization that creates urban farms in schools through vegetable gardens, plant-based cooking lessons, hydroponic labs, and classes on healthy eating, supports the physical aspect of self-care through promoting a healthy lifestyle in communities that may be healthy food deserts. These practices expand the idea of self-care as a schoolwide culture. The school thoughtfully and purposefully models and commits by creating access to self-care for all constituents of the school community through dedicated programming, resources, and time.

As school leaders, you are caregivers of the school community. While you engage in self-care practices yourself, you should also create a culture where self-care is valued and provide opportunities for others to practice it.

Conclusion

In this chapter, we discussed the significance of self-care as an effective leadership competency. We learned from Dawn's experiences with self-care and self-neglect and the impact on her mental, emotional, and physical health and well-being. The ways you self-regulate, express, or restrain emotion impact the ways others receive and interact with you, your actions, and ultimately outcomes for students.

In the next chapter, we will investigate how self-care and, specifically, self-awareness connect to creating a racial autobiography, a process Mark uses in his support and professional development of school leaders. After engaging in the following reflective questions, please see the suggested "Potential Action Steps" reproducible (page 65) to help you implement these protocols in your school.

Questions for Reflection and Discussion

Please reflect on the following questions, alone or in a book discussion group, to consider the chapter content and your current and future leadership practices.

1. What new knowledge did you gain about self-care?
2. What experiences, beliefs, or models of self-care did you experience growing up? How has that impacted your beliefs about self-care?
3. Upon reflecting on your own workload and physical and mental well-being, is there a specific area in your own life where you think you may need more attention to self-care?
4. What barriers are there to improving your own self-care practices?

Self-Care Reflection

Reflect on your current practices regarding self-care and then brainstorm ways you can improve these practices.

Self-Care Area	My Current Practices	Actions to Improve My Practices
Physical: Caring for the physical body		
Professional: Reducing work-related risks		
Relational: Nourishing interpersonal relationships		
Emotional: Mitigating negative emotional experiences and creating positive emotional experiences		
Psychological: Attending to intellectual needs		
Spiritual: Reflecting on the inner self and relationship to the universe		

Source: Butler, L. D., Mercer, K. A., McClain-Meeder, K., Horne, D. M., & Dudley, M. (2019). Six domains of self-care: Attending to the whole person. *Journal of Human Behavior in the Social Environment, 29*(1), 107–124.

Potential Action Steps

In the potential action steps for chapter 3, you have the opportunity to deepen the work and operationalize a practice or practices you and your team would like to begin with. Choose as many or as few as you are able. Consider quality over quantity and think of these possible action steps as opportunities to grow, strengthen, and build on as opposed to steps to take all at once.

- Use the "Self-Care Reflection" reproducible (page 64) to pinpoint the areas you want to focus on to build consistency.
- Review the suggested strategies you can incorporate into areas of your life where you need more self-care.
- Identify colleagues, family members, or friends who might join you on this journey to self-care as accountability partners.
- Start small and determine with your team where you might co-create opportunities for self-care practices for your staff, students, and families to begin incorporating self-care as a part of the school culture.

Note: Remember, this work will take time. It is continuous and ongoing. Pace yourself according to the needs of your community.

4

Engaging in Racial Reflection

In this chapter, we will discuss the importance of racial reflection, specifically, Mark's racial autobiography process, which is a central part of the self-awareness component of CRASEL. We will also discuss other methods of racial reflection, both individual and collaborative. We will hear about Dawn's experience creating her own racial autobiography as a student of Mark, and how she shared the process with her school community. We will describe the components of these processes and the benefit of engaging in these practices as a culturally responsive school leader. We will learn how the TMALS community embraced this culturally responsive process as a strategy to interrupt oppression and build equity, connectedness, belonging, and collective awareness.

Mark A. Gooden (2021) explains, "discussing school leadership in the absence of race is like building a house absent a foundation. While that house may stay upright for some time, it will be ill-prepared to withstand the strong winds of change" (p. 33). The racial autobiography is "a narrative written to explore how race has manifested in one's life" (Gooden, 2021, p. 34). This deeper level of self-awareness in our increasingly multicultural society is a competency leaders will need to authentically engage their school communities in, in a way that centers a culturally responsive approach. As lead learners, principals should be willing to interrogate their own perceptions and the impact of their perspectives, experiences, and beliefs on those they lead.

Words From a Principal

As a student in Dr. Gooden's doctoral class at Teachers College, Columbia University, along with other school and district leaders, I had the opportunity to engage in a racial autobiography project. Dr. Gooden challenged us to reflect on our earliest experiences with race. We shared those experiences with our peers and began self-reflecting on how those experiences impacted our perspectives and actions personally and professionally.

I recalled some things I had not thought about in many years. Eventually I was able to make the connection between how those earlier experiences, some positive and some negative, made me the leader I am today. I reflected on the sense of pride my family instilled in me around my racial identity and culture as a young child. I remembered experiences I had in school with teachers who were culturally responsive without knowing or understanding that term at the time. I remembered the nuns and brothers at St. Gabriel's School in Queens, New York, having high expectations for all of us.

I also remembered troubling negative experiences, such as being called the N-word on various occasions and feeling the same impact in the current moment that I had when it happened first, more than thirty years prior. I recalled and detailed the times it happened again after that in my childhood. I had not thought about these experiences in a long time, and it was challenging to detail them in writing and feel the same trauma that I felt then as if it had just happened. It made me think about racially violent events going on in the world and the experiences my students were having.

I wanted to share this powerful experience with my teachers to help ground them even deeper in our culturally responsive purpose. The experience fortified my purpose in ensuring we were creating positive racial experiences for our students, knowing that these experiences would be as long lasting for them as they were for me. I understood after this experience that, without knowing it, our earliest experiences surface in the way we teach and lead. They can cause us to hold trauma, beliefs, fears, and at times misinformation about race that impact how we interact with one another. As I did with my classmates in Dr. Gooden's class, I shared my autobiography with my staff, and it was emotional and cathartic. I have worked with some of my teachers for more than twenty years as colleagues. Despite the length of time some of the staff worked together, we learned things about one another that we would have never known had we not engaged in this practice.

I modified the process for my staff and had them create visual racial autobiography presentations with pictures, links, and resources. It created connections and a sense of belonging. There were very few teachers who were not comfortable sharing their experiences with race and their racial autobiographies, but allowing people to enter where they can has been impactful. I could not have anticipated how the process would grow into one that is now schoolwide and includes not only staff but also students and families. I also had the opportunity to share the process with a few of my colleagues who were able to implement the practice with their staff with a similar positive impact on the community.

Knowing that we have past racial experiences that impact us today can serve as a tool. This process doesn't eradicate the challenges with race, but where we see our own biases and fears coming up, we can understand where they all came from and interrupt them. Where we may have been racially isolated and devoid of experiences with diversity, we can seek to rectify. This process is not an easy one, but it is worth the effort. You can also find joy in the process. Learning more about one another and sharing pieces of ourselves in a caring community makes our connection and level of trust even stronger.

Words From a Professor

When I initially started as an assistant professor in 2001, I had not written a racial autobiography. I felt that race was a part of my research because of how I identified at the time, which was simply as a Black man. Though I had served as a mathematics teacher for four years, my first higher education position was at the University of Cincinnati. I recall that when I was interviewing for the job, I wondered whether the College of Education or the university had gotten involved with the recent deaths of Black men at the hands of police in the city. Timothy Thomas, an unarmed nineteen-year-old Black man, had been murdered with a fatal shot to the back, and it set off four days of civil protests in the city, resulting in about a thousand people being arrested. Stephen Roach, the offending Cincinnati police officer, was charged with negligent homicide but eventually acquitted.

I felt uneasy as I formulated the question in my mind, but I still decided to ask my future colleagues whether there had been a plan to respond to the shooting and the community response, or to connect it to education, as these events were all happening around the time I was interviewing. The question appeared to surprise and confuse several people in the room. The response did not surprise me. It was something like "We have not done anything to address this issue, but we would fully support your interest in addressing it."

At the time, I felt a need to learn more and engage in the process of studying race and how the lives of Black people were impacted in obvious and not-so-obvious ways by education. I felt as if it were a struggle to bring race into the conversation at that interview, especially as most people present appeared to feel race or racism on display in the city was not their issue. Emotionally, they were disconnected from the experience of Timothy Thomas, his family, and his community. That bothered me. I wanted to get better at that process of deepening engagement, especially relative to empathy, so it would become clear it was everyone's issue. I wanted to better articulate how I was impacted emotionally by an occurrence that so few of my future colleagues had connected with at all.

I became more proficient at studying the impact of race. For example, I studied critical race theory to better understand the powerful connections between law, structural inequities, and opportunities. I had the privilege to publish a research article after studying with an African American principal fighting to create equitable opportunities for students of a predominantly Black urban high school. All these experiences helped me to grow and deepen my understanding of the requirement to face racial inequity directly. However, I was still developing my ability to connect emotionally and experientially with racial equity work in a way that taught me and enhanced how I taught others.

Something happened when I better understood the power of engaging in racial reflections and exploring how they excited me but also made me nervous. Though I would later take a professional development workshop on emotional intelligence, it would be some years before I made the connection that interrogating race is enhanced by openly exploring and properly processing a range of emotions—yet so many avoid including emotions in teaching and learning altogether. I wondered what the best way would be to endorse emotional engagement on race, a topic that appeared to raise so much anxiety with so many students.

In this book, I share how that early learning helped me to support principals like Dawn as they incorporate emotional intelligence in a range of equity explorations. Engaging in research that centers race and culture helped me become a better professor and leader, as I learned to apply this lens to a range of tasks and experiences in my role as a researcher, teacher, and academic leader. For example, I have invited students to explore race to gain a deeper understanding of how they see themselves and how they view the world as a first step to changing that world. After all, it's a good idea to start this conversation of self-perception early in the leading process.

RELATE AND REFLECT
• Can you relate to Dawn's emotional reaction to reflecting on her earliest experiences with race? How?
• Can you relate to the challenges Mark experienced in learning to engage in conversations about race and equity with those who don't see it as an issue? How?
• Do you see the racial reflection practice as beneficial for you personally? In what ways?
• How do you think sharing your experiences with your staff could benefit your relationship with them?

The Racial Autobiography: A Culturally Responsive Leadership Practice

The general process for a racial autobiography is as follows. Consider how you would describe yourself racially and write it down. What were your earliest experiences with race? Then write responses to the following questions. What would you say is the largest racial group in the United States for teachers? For school leaders? Are you part of that group? When you consider your work, does race matter in any significant way? Don't be afraid to really go into detail in your responses.

Think for a moment about personal racial experiences occurring at different points in your life. Try very hard to recall some of your earliest experiences with race, noting when they happened in your life, including whether they occurred in elementary, middle, or high school. Were there instances in postsecondary education that come to mind that you can write about? Organize these points in chronological order and aim to weave them together into a narrative by explaining how race came up in your life and the world around you, what happened when it did, and how you responded. If there was tension or conflict, be sure to share that and how it was resolved. Finally, consider what lessons you gleaned from these experiences. The reproducible "Racial Autobiography Reflection" tool at the end of the chapter (page 80) can help you start or reflect on your own racial autobiography and racial reflection process.

Gooden (2021) defines the racial autobiography as "a narrative written to explore how race has manifested in one's life—that can support a leader's goal of becoming antiracist" (p. 33). Caprice D. Hollins and Ilsa M. Govan (2015) provide working definitions for race and ethnicity and explain that there is no biological basis for racial categories. They show that scientific research identifies race as a social and political construct based on physical traits such as skin and eye color and hair texture. And although race is not biological, it is experiential in that perceptions, beliefs, access to opportunities, and stereotypes prevent us from escaping the reality of race. According to the 2022 NCES report:

> In fall 2020, of the 49.4 million students enrolled in public elementary and secondary schools, 46 percent were White (a decrease from 54 percent in 2009), 15 percent were Black (a decrease from 17 percent), and 28 percent were Hispanic (an increase from 22 percent). (Irwin et al., 2022, p. 12)

Those who study changing demographics predict students of color will be the majority of the U.S. student population by 2035 (Williams-Wyche, Fergus, & Djurovich, 2016). However, NCES has confirmed that 56 percent of public-school students are of color as of fall 2022 (Irwin et al., 2022). These demographic changes require that teachers and leaders be better prepared to serve a more diverse population. More and more, leaders will need to co-create communities of belonging and connectedness for their students and families. Teacher and principal preparation programs will need to better prepare educators for the schools they will lead and teach in and should position them to better serve the needs of their students in ways that will allow them to thrive. Leader and educator biases and beliefs impact the ways they lead and directly influence the level of expectations they hold. Gooden (2021) asserts that the racial autobiography experience can expose the social construct of race in a way that allows participants to examine their own beliefs and the impact of their perspectives on their actions and relationships with those of other races.

Mark A. Gooden and Ann O'Doherty (2015) created a racial self-reflective and trust-building process, Building a Community of Trust Through Racial Awareness, in which they engage participants in a series of reflective experiences, inquiry protocols, article studies, conversations, and more designed to help participants examine their experiences and perspectives around race. The process also prepares facilitators to support participants in the expected variety of emotions and reactions they may experience during the process. The goal of the process is to engage participants in a transformational experience that will lead to empowerment and motivation for change (Gooden & Dantley, 2012). Participants respond to writing prompts about their racial experiences by journaling about their racial experiences and their leadership practices that involve race. They have the opportunity through the experience to build their capacity and understanding around race by engaging with research. Notions of White privilege are also interrogated as part of the racial autobiography process and racial awareness reflection.

The teaching profession being predominantly White has an undeniable impact on students of color (Gooden & O'Doherty, 2015). Gooden and O'Doherty (2015) convey that the "power and privilege of Whiteness is most apparent and oftentimes suffocating to Black students, who struggled to 'cope' with the microaggressions and the additional cognitive load of working against negative stereotypes in a dominant culture" (p. 242). Without a process to acknowledge and interrupt these potentially damaging perceptions that negatively impact students of color, teachers run the risk of consciously or unconsciously creating classroom experiences and interactions that are harmful to students. Some of these actions include teachers failing to meet students' needs due to low expectations, stereotyping students, othering or invisibilizing students, using microaggressions against students, disparate disciplinary consequences for students, and more.

You are ultimately responsible for the expectations around your teachers' approaches in your school and the climate and culture fostered by the school. It is therefore your responsibility to build the reflective capacity of your teachers. As Dawn shared in her reflection on engaging in the racial autobiography process herself and sharing her work with her staff, she modeled the vulnerability and self-growth that allowed her staff a safe space to begin their learning. She also attests to how her active participation as lead learner helped to build trust in the community.

Khalifa and colleagues (2016) establish the first component of culturally responsive school leadership as critical self-awareness, defined as "the notion that the leader needed to have an awareness of self and his/her values, beliefs, and/or dispositions when it came to serving poor children of color" (p. 1280). The transformative aspect of the racial autobiography positions you as an advocate for change in your community and an antiracist leader who can interrupt policies and practices that marginalize your students and families. It also gives those in homogeneous, racially isolated communities an opportunity to expand their knowledge and awareness and dispel racial stereotypes and biases that can cause fear. Sadly, racial violence can occur because of fear and misinformation. You can shift this trauma for your students by starting with investigating your own beliefs and dispositions that threaten to maintain racial discrimination in your schools.

As you read about the racial autobiography process, participants are asked to reflect on their earliest experiences with race. As Dawn also experienced when embarking on this with her staff, themes emerged. Gooden and O'Doherty (2015) find in their research of the racial autobiography process that participants' early racial reflections fall into three categories: "racial isolation or racial separation, influence of family members, and discomfort when in the minority" (p. 234). They also note the progress made in several instances "where aspiring leaders (teachers), particularly White study participants, grappled with how they had previously ignored race, denied that race existed, or believed racism did not have a place in modern society" (Gooden & O'Doherty, 2015, p. 242).

The awareness leaders and educators gain as a result of this practice can lead to direct action that enhances the academic achievement and experiences of students of color. In their book *Five Practices for Equity-Focused School Leadership*, Sharon I. Radd and colleagues (2021) provide a guideline for how leaders can interrupt negative practices and attitudes and note that "good leaders understand this reality and courageously prepare to address it by first becoming more racially aware to surface their assumptions

> *The transformative aspect of the racial autobiography positions you as an advocate for change in your community and an antiracist leader who can interrupt policies and practices that marginalize your students and families.*

and biases, with the goal of developing a critical consciousness" (p. 63). Radd and colleagues (2021) outline the process for engaging in the racial experiences conversation, crafting one's individual story, and creating a personal timeline reflecting on race. The six practices explored in their text include (1) centering equity, (2) prioritizing equity leadership, (3) preparing for equity, (4) developing equity leadership teams, (5) building equity-focused systems, and (6) sustaining equity. Their book can serve as a professional workbook for leaders in developing each of these equity practices.

The Importance of Racial Reflection

In their seminal work that impacted scholarship across the field of education, Geneva Gay and Kipchoge Kirkland (2003) highlight critical consciousness as a competency in cultural responsiveness, conveying the need for educators to know themselves, know the lives and context of their students, and as a result interrogate their beliefs and dispositions regularly in service of their students. Aiesha T. Lee and Natoya Hill Haskins (2022) agree that critical consciousness is culturally responsive and necessary to fully support others. Khalifa and colleagues' (2016) literature synthesis establishes the concept of critical consciousness as a culturally responsive leadership component. Gay and Kirkland (2003) outline cultural responsiveness as linked to self-awareness is:

> based on the premises that (a) multicultural education and educational equity and excellence are deeply interconnected; (b) teacher accountability involves being more self-conscious, critical, and analytical of one's own teaching beliefs and behaviors; and (c) teachers need to develop deeper knowledge and consciousness about what is to be taught, how, and to whom. (p. 181)

In chapter 3 (page 53), we learned about the need for emotional self-awareness as it impacts not only your own quality of life but also those you interact with. The racial autobiography and racial reflection can foster this critical consciousness, which is a needed aspect of effective culturally responsive leadership. To be critically conscious, you must have a sense of self-awareness and an understanding of the sociopolitical context of the students you serve. Tyrone C. Howard (2019) notes that "critical reflection and self-assessment" in combination with developing cultural competence will allow teachers and leaders to acknowledge how their biases and "deficit-based notions of culturally diverse students, distorted views of low-income communities, and negative perceptions of students' families" can be interrupted (p. 113).

You must use your critically conscious understanding to create nurturing environments for all students, including those who have been excluded or mistreated based on race and culture. The self-reflective aspect of leadership should bring leaders to an awareness of any racist policies and practices that occur within the school so they may advocate and interrupt those practices (Khalifa et al., 2016). Howard (2019) asks of educators in their critical self-reflection, "Does 'who I am' contribute to the underachievement of students who are not like me?" (p. 113). For you, modeling and leading a school community where self-reflection is ongoing and supported allows for cyclical, needed change. Knowing students and their families well and acknowledging where learning more about them is needed is part of the purpose of critical self-reflection.

This self-reflection should lead you to action and advocacy. Understanding your positionality in relation to power, privilege, oppression, and the community you serve should lead to critical decision making on behalf of students and their families. Chinwe Esimai (2018) notes that although self-awareness is accepted as an important leadership competency, many leaders lack this capacity. It is your responsibility to nurture growth not only within students but also in the staff. Meeting teachers where they are and supporting their growth and capacity building are important parts of increasing success for students. Engaging your staff in a self-reflective practice that can impact the quality of teaching and learning in the school builds growth (Bray, Gunsalus, Luckman, Burbules, & Easter, 2019).

There are opportunities in this process for leaders to build cohesive common understandings of key terms such as *race*, *ethnicity*, and *culture*. You can also build your staff's cultural competency through article studies of leading research in the fields of cultural responsiveness and racial equity. While teachers are journaling, reflecting, and acknowledging their own beliefs and dispositions, they can also learn how biases can surface in the classroom and school and what steps they can take to restore balance. This will allow them the capacity to address and interrupt harm they may be unintentionally causing through their decision making or their interactions with students and families.

Racial reflection is the beginning and should lead to growth, advocacy, and change; remember, that's how we started this chapter. Stefanie LuVenia Marshall and Muhammad A. Khalifa (2018) discuss the movement from self-awareness and critical reflection to the unlearning of harmful practices once educators discover how their biases are negatively surfacing in their work. Freire (1973) in his seminal work defined critical consciousness as "learning to perceive social, political, and economic contradictions and to take action against the oppressive elements of reality" (p. 4). Next, we share how a team moved from reflection to practice by using the information from their reflections and an audit of the school's policies and practices in the creation of a schoolwide vision for racial equity.

A Schoolwide Vision for Racial Equity

The self-reflective critical consciousness that happens on the personal level should impact the individual's shift in thinking and practice. Self-reflection should also happen for the school community itself. Collectively and collaboratively, there is an opportunity for the school to analyze itself, its policies, its beliefs, its practices, how students feel in the space, and how different constituents such as parents and caregivers receive the school. This school reflection can happen through a process of co-creating a vision for racial equity.

TMALS values collaborative professional learning, and as such engaged in several opportunities to participate in learning collaboratives. One of the processes they experienced was creating their vision for racial equity. As part of this process, the school team, including the principal, assistant principal, teachers, and support staff, engaged in an audit of their policies and practices. They selected a mix of qualitative and quantitative data to examine including grading policies, discipline data, proficiency data, student work, special education data, programming, access to advanced courses, and so on. This collective reflection led to subsequent action planning to address any problem areas where racial disparities surfaced. The data made the process concrete, with an ultimate expectation for a change in any discriminatory policy or practice to ensure equity. The TMALS team engaging in this work collectively was key to its success.

The steps TMALS engaged in to create the vision for racial equity include the following.

1. School teams studied the first chapter of Zaretta Hammond's (2015) book *Culturally Responsive Teaching and the Brain* to learn how to create equitable school communities.

2. Teams created or adopted norms. They studied Glenn E. Singleton and Cyndie Hays's (2008) four agreements of courageous conversations from their book chapter "Beginning Courageous Conversations About Race."

3. Teams collaborated with all stakeholders, including administrators, staff, parents, caregivers, partners, and students, to envision and brainstorm what their school would look like, feel like, and sound like in its ideal state of racial equity.

4. After gathering stakeholders' feedback on an ideal environment of racial equity, the lead team examined the findings, looking for patterns. The team discussed the findings.

5. The lead team began crafting the racial equity vision statement. The statement included what specific actions various constituents would

take to create racial equity within the school community and what impact those actions would have on students and outcomes.

6. The lead team shared the draft statement with all stakeholders for any additional feedback before finalizing the statement.
7. The lead team gathered at least three pieces of learning-focused quantitative and qualitative data to examine for lack of equitable practices. The team members reviewed the data individually prior to discussing.
8. The lead team came to a collective decision on one area to address.
9. Using the school's newly created vision for racial equity, the team examined the data against the expectations of the vision.
10. The team used a problem-of-practice protocol to address changing the policy or practice. Visit the Center for Leadership and Educational Equity (www.schoolreforminitiative.org/protocols) for possible protocols.
11. This full practice should include transparency and regular communication with the school community.

The following statement is a sample vision for racial equity.

> One hundred percent of our students experience consistent support, are known well by at least one adult, and are heard and feel physically and emotionally safe in our school. This is consistent across all races, genders, and socioeconomic statuses. These experiences allow students to thrive socially and academically. As a school leader, I will serve as a caring advocate for all students, staff, and families. I will model and prioritize the physical and emotional wellness of all members of the school community while also prioritizing student academic success. Our approach to learning will include self-care, student and family support systems, and culturally responsive and affirming SEL curricula that reflect the identities of the students and diverse cultures. Teachers will prioritize student physical, social, and emotional wellness through daily SEL practices, with academic support that meets student needs. Teachers will also seek to know their students and families well.

School leaders can engage their school community in the process of co-creating a collective schoolwide vision for racial equity. It is important to include representation from all constituent groups in the process—leaders, teachers, support staff, parents, partners, and students. This will include all perspectives in the vision. The vision should be based not only on perspectives, but also on the actual experiences of members of the school community as well as school data such as academic, attendance, school culture, suspensions, and incident data. At the school's highest ideal, who do they aspire to be as a community if they achieve true racial equity? This vision serves as a gauge and a guiding light as the school creates and implements policies and practices.

Words From a Principal

TMALS was created on the premise of cultural responsiveness and social justice. Implemented by Dr. Sean L. Davenport, the founding principal of the school, the vision for racial justice has always been a part of the TMALS mission. Over the years, the practices have deepened, beginning with engaging students in texts and topics that reflect their own culture and the cultures of others. Creating opportunities for students to see models of excellence who look like them is key. Curriculum, text, celebrations, and historical studies, as well as engagement in current social justice activities, are staples at TMALS.

Although teachers regularly engaged students in topics of race and culture, there was not a practice or process for the staff to explore and share their own cultures with their students. The racial autobiography process, re-envisioned by the principal as a visual interactive presentation shared across the school, began with the school's principal sharing her own visual racial autobiography presentation with staff. After sharing her own racial and ethnic identity statements, she engaged staff in a racial reflection and the creation of their own statements.

The transparency of the leader showing vulnerability fostered the safe space staff needed to create and share their own experiences and presentations. The staff journaled and then shared their earliest experiences with race in small groups, and after that, those who were ready shared their experiences with the full group. Most staff said their earliest experiences were as children in school. Several teachers recalled that the experiences were traumatizing and long lasting. They reflected on things from their past that they had not thought about in years but were experiences they would never forget. The racial trauma teachers had experienced was evident.

The fact that most of the experiences occurred in school led the team to understand the need to create positive experiences around race for children in school. Teachers then shared their presentations with students and encouraged students to collaborate with their families in creating their own racial and ethnic identity statements and visual racial autobiographies. They embedded links and resources so the presentations also became opportunities for extended learning in the wide variety of cultures present in the school community. Staff prominently displayed their visual autobiographies in the school for all to see.

Students enjoy learning more about the lives of their teachers and leaders. Doing so humanizes teachers and leaders in the eyes of students and families and builds connectedness and a sense of belonging across the community.

Conclusion

In this chapter, we presented instructions on how to complete a racial autobiography and examined the benefits of principals expanding the racial autobiography process to include other leaders (Gooden, 2021). We heard about Dawn's experience with the racial autobiography, and how and why she decided to share the practice with her staff. Creating a racial autobiography is an act of building self-awareness. There is a need for self-care in reflecting on our experiences with race that may have been traumatizing. It's important that we work toward understanding how our experiences with race impact how we lead and interact with others. We delved into the process of creating a schoolwide vision for racial equity and how to use this vision to ensure policies and practices are equitable across the school community.

In the next chapter, we will dig into relationship building in the school community. Through a collective and collaborative process, built on trust and a common goal, we outline how leaders can co-create a vision through teacher leadership, student agency, and family empowerment. You cannot create and execute a vision on your own. There should be a collective effort that all stakeholders create and own. When the members of the community collaborate, there is a sense of accountability and responsibility in continuing and keeping the work alive. After engaging in the following reflective questions, please see the suggested "Potential Action Steps" reproducible (page 81) to help you implement these protocols in your school.

Questions for Reflection and Discussion

Please reflect on the following questions, alone or in a book discussion group, to consider the chapter content and your current and future leadership practices.

1. Upon reflecting on your own initial racial reflection and your earliest experiences with race, what discoveries have you made about how your earlier experiences impact your leadership today?

2. What barriers do you anticipate in creating or sharing your racial autobiography?

3. What are your thoughts about the connections between self-awareness and racial reflection?

4. What experiences have you had that may cause you to hold perceptions about a specific demographic of students in your care?

5. If your perceptions negatively impact how you lead or interact with this particular group of students, how might you learn more about them and their sociopolitical context in order to serve them better?

Racial Autobiography Reflection

Use this reflection tool to help you begin or further reflect on your racial autobiography and racial reflection process.

Who are you racially and ethnically? Write a statement.	
Describe one of your earliest memories of race. When did you become aware of race as a construct?	
Was this experience positive or negative?	
When and where did this occur? How old were you?	
In what ways might this memory influence your current perspective? How does this manifest in your leadership?	

The Change You Want to See © 2025 Solution Tree Press • SolutionTree.com
Visit **go.SolutionTree.com/leadership** to download this free reproducible.

Potential Action Steps

In the potential action steps for chapter 4, you have the opportunity to deepen the work and operationalize a practice or practices you and your team would like to begin with. Choose as many or as few as you are able. Consider quality over quantity and think of these possible action steps as opportunities to grow, strengthen, and build on as opposed to steps to take all at once.

- Engage in your own racial autobiography.
- Read Mark Anthony Gooden's (2021) article "Why Every Principal Should Write a Racial Autobiography."
- Create a slide presentation to accompany your racial autobiography that you can share with your staff. Be prepared to share your process and experience with your staff and the importance of engaging in this practice.
- Create a core racial equity vision team to facilitate the co-creation of your school's vision for racial equity.
- Determine the ways you will, in collaboration with your core team, gather the perspectives and voices of all stakeholders in the school community.
- Identify patterns across stakeholders in the creation of the vision.
- Share the draft vision with all stakeholders for feedback, then finalize and reshare the vision.
- Keep the vision at the forefront and utilize it when making decisions, creating schoolwide policies, examining instruction, and assessing student achievement.
- Make adjustments in policies and practices where needed to align with the vision. Exercise transparency with any adjustments made.

Note: Remember, this work will take time. It is continuous and ongoing. Pace yourself according to the needs of your community.

Reference

Gooden, M. A. (2021). Why every principal should write a racial autobiography. *Educational Leadership, 78*(7), 32–37.

5

Building School and Community Relationships

This chapter details the second step of the CRASEL framework, which is building relationships in school and community. Effective school leaders do not work in isolation. Through building teacher leaderships, providing opportunities for collaboration, facilitating student and staff agency, and cultivating family empowerment, leaders can collectively co-liberate their school communities. Through an inclusive approach to leadership, all members of the school community have opportunities for input and are not only receivers of information but also active participants in continuing and promoting the school's mission, vision, and goals. In this way, all members of the community are accountable for student success and work together equitably toward a common goal. In this chapter, we will outline the purpose and need for leaders to build trusting relationships with and within their school communities.

Words From a Principal

About four years into my time as a principal, I had the opportunity to join the Cahn Fellowship as a fellow. The Cahn Fellowship provides professional learning and development for principals of inner-city schools who are nominated based on their success and accomplishments as school leaders. With the support of mentors, the principals learn advanced leadership strategies in cohorts of leaders from across the

United States, developing areas of focus to explore and improve within their own school communities. Through its alumni organization, these leaders are able to participate in an enduring culture of fellowship and collective leadership development. The Cahn Fellowship is a prestigious organization, well known for its approach to leadership development. Even after many years of my own time as a Cahn fellow, when I meet other principals who share the experience, I feel a sense of kinship with them.

As part of the fellowship, I was able to select a Cahn ally. An ally is a person on your staff in whom you see leadership potential who will participate in the fellowship alongside you, developing their leadership skills and capacity. I was fortunate enough to have two Cahn allies from my school, Siobhan Mould and Kerri Seow. Both were strong teachers in whom I saw great potential—not only for their skills as educators, but also for their capacity to build relationships with their students, families, and colleagues. They were both models of the vision of our school, active participants who knew the value of working collectively toward success. Their classrooms were caring communities, and I knew this was primarily because of them.

When it was time to decide on the problem of practice that we would work on as a team, I had a plan for advancing academic achievement. After sharing my plan with my allies (a plan I created on my own), they compassionately shared that there was a bigger issue than academic achievement that we needed to address. They shared the lack of trust that existed among our staff, who worked in silos, formed cliques, gossiped, and lacked cohesion. This was difficult to hear. I had noticed this myself, but thought if we just focused on the students, that would drive the work. They were transparent, and through the support of my mentor at Cahn, Dr. Ellie Drago-Severson, we created a trust-building project that I will outline later in the chapter (page 91).

As part of the project, we conducted a series of surveys in which I asked very specific questions about how my staff were receiving my leadership. There was a pattern in the responses about people not feeling included in decision making. I will never forget one of the responses: "This is a one-man ship." I knew that the "one man" was me. After reflecting, I saw how I had been making decisions on my own and then wondering why people didn't feel accountable. They weren't accountable because they had no part in creating the vision. I thought I was exercising leadership by making decisions and delivering directives. I had not worked to be inclusive; I was working in isolation, and since that was what I modeled, the staff were operating the same way.

Without relationships and trust, educators cannot effectively collaborate to support their students, share best practices, or offer constructive feedback toward their collective growth. I thanked my allies for their honesty and their trust as they shared this difficult truth. This realization and ownership of the truth allowed me to *create a plan forward along with my allies to create a culture of collaboration, feedback, and compassion.*

Words From a Professor

Leadership literature concedes that while leadership endeavors might start with the principal, courageous and committed principals recognize the job's increased complexity and the pitfalls that come with trying to do it all alone. Yes, the principalship is a lonely job, and it can be scary for leaders to include others in the decision-making process, especially when, as building leaders, they will be solely responsible for the quality of the work. Even though that kind of accountability thinking is problematic as a cultural norm, it still pervades many districts and contributes to some leaders' reluctance in letting others come on board.

However, I would like to propose that when we develop leaders, we do so by establishing teaming protocols and processes that remind leaders of the importance of working together. That approach increases the likelihood that principals will be more open to searching for talent within the building and including those folks in the leadership process. Ultimately, this is part of Dawn's process. It is also important that as principal she collected data to confirm what was already a suspicion of hers—that perhaps her leadership was leaving little room for input. Though leaders may be exposed in their preparation programs to ways to build and maintain teams, they still have to muster the courage to put this work into action at their schools. They must also determine how to do that work, especially when managing the many emotions that come with doing culturally responsive and equity-centered work.

First, leaders should be clear that they plan to develop a team of people that can support the work of the equity-focused principalship (Radd et al., 2021). Alternatively, they can commit to center the equity work within an already-established team structure within the school. At this point in the book, leaders will be familiar with the CRASEL framework, but you should ensure that all team members are as well. Second, as we have noted, engaging in rich processes like completing racial autobiographies and sharing them is one way that trust building can occur. Finally, building leaders must be open to employing different strategies and structures for leading. Ironically, when Dawn collected her data, she heard "one-man ship" in reference to her style of leadership even though she is obviously a woman. Incidentally, this phrase brings up the "great man theory" in leadership that supports the same philosophy that the leader must do it all.

By distributing the responsibilities, the leader will begin to build trust. By restructuring the way the school is run and how staff members (besides the principal) lead different tasks, the leader will start to build capacity. Most certainly, there will be mistakes made and lessons learned along the way, but the result will establish deeper relationships and roots for going forward in making the school more equitable and emotionally centered.

> **RELATE AND REFLECT**
> - Do you relate to Dawn's experience as a leader needing to build relationships? How so?
> - Do you see the need for leaders to create opportunities for relationship and trust building? In what ways?
> - How have you experienced trust and relationship building in your school community?
> - How do you think asking your staff for honest feedback on your leadership might benefit your leadership?

The Importance of Relational Trust

The theme of relationships has been dominant throughout this book. It surfaces in almost every area of culturally responsive and affirming social-emotional leadership. This is reflected in relationships with oneself through critical self-reflection, and with those in your school and community. Your ability to engage in positive and collaborative relationships in all aspects of leadership is key. Anthony S. Bryk and Barbara Schneider (2002) define *relational trust* as the day-to-day interactions that happen in a school community where the members depend on one another and collectively work on school improvements. They outline the components that build relational trust as respect, personal regard for others, competence, and integrity. Through these components, individuals listen to one another, value one another's opinions, go above and beyond in their support of one another, fulfill their professional duties with a sense of responsibility toward one another, and feel a moral obligation to act with integrity and consistency.

You should be a model of the relationships you seek to build in your school communities. This sense of community and relational trust is necessary in collective efforts toward achieving the school's vision for success. In earlier chapters, we discussed critical self-reflection, the racial autobiography, and co-creating visions for racial equity. All these processes include a level of vulnerability and transparency that is only possible in a community where there is trust and relationships are strong. People are less willing to publicly learn, share parts of themselves, and work on areas of challenge in environments where they do not feel emotionally safe. Dawn's vulnerability in sharing her own racial autobiography with her staff before engaging them in the practice helped to create a level of trust that allowed them to engage and face their fears around the process.

Addressing issues of race and culture can be challenging, and although trust alone does not solve every challenge, it creates the connectedness that motivates the community to tackle challenges together for the success of all involved. Relational trust fosters connectedness and belongingness, resulting in the safe environment educators, students, and families need to openly share. When leaders and educators feel a connected, moral, responsible relationship with the students and families they serve and with one another, their efforts toward ensuring that all are valued, included, and seen are culturally responsive.

Bodunrin O. Banwo, Muhammad Khalifa, and Karen Seashore Louis (2022) examine the effect of trust on culturally responsive school leadership through case studies that reveal that the honesty, compassion, and fairness that trust and relationship building creates are crucial to creating equitable school environments free of bias and mistreatment. Similar to the trust required for cultural responsiveness in SEL, the need to see and know students well and the need for students and families to trust educators and leaders create a sense of emotional safety in a trusting environment.

> *You should be a model of the relationships you seek to build in your school communities.*

Emotionally safe environments are not automatic; they take time and trust to create and maintain. The daily interactions that reflect relational trust need care.

Just as building trust takes time, trust can be broken whether intentionally or unintentionally in one short interaction. And often, once the trust is broken, it is never given the time and care to repair. Relational trust and the daily interactions that occur within a school community require that we care for one another's emotions. We should care so much about the emotions of others that we always exercise care with our words and actions. And although conflict is a natural occurrence in any relationship, when there is trust, there is an effort to listen and to repair any harm that has occurred.

How to Strengthen Community Relationships

The CRASEL framework provides actions leaders can take to build relationships with all members of the school community to create a sense of community, collective responsibility, agency, and inclusivity (Brooks DeCosta, 2020). The components of the community and relationship-building areas of the framework include the following actions.

- Engage in supportive, understanding, and positive communication.
- Take the perspectives of others with empathy.
- Find connections between school and community.
- Connect directly with students, staff, families, and community.

We discuss these actions in detail in the following sections.

Engage in Supportive, Understanding, and Positive Communication

Effective communication impacts the quality of leadership. When leaders communicate frequently, transparently, and in supportive ways, the members of the school community feel more connected to and trusting of the leader. You can create supportive, understanding, and positive communication with students, families, and staff through regular and frequent communication streams. The following are some examples of how to do this.

- Create an avenue for staff to share their feedback with school leaders throughout the school year, either through check-in meetings or through surveys. This is key to fostering dialogue and input in ways that allow staff to feel included and well informed. When leaders are transparent and model how to receive feedback from staff, it builds the trust needed for positive communication.

- Communicate regularly and openly with students through town hall discussions and smaller focus group conversations with students. This builds connection and trust between the leader and their students. It is also a source of knowledge and awareness for the leader on what students are experiencing daily.

- Engage in frequent, multifaceted, multimedia, regular communication with families to foster a supportive environment. Be responsive to family needs, requests, and correspondence in a timely manner to create supportive, positive communication. Don't allow problems and concerns to fester; always seek to restore and respond with urgency.

- Create structures for students and families to share their thoughts, needs, concerns, and experiences. This is important for leaders to keep a pulse on the community to make responsive adjustments to school policies and practices as needed.

Take the Perspectives of Others With Empathy

Emotionally intelligent leaders hold the capacity for perspective taking and empathy. Leaders who have strong relationships with their school communities lead with emotional intelligence. These leaders are also culturally responsive and know their students and families well, and they know their experiences in the community. When you are unable to practice perspective taking, there is a disconnect and lack of knowledge, empathy, and compassion on your part regarding the experiences of those you serve. Leaders can practice perspective taking and empathy in various ways, such as the following.

- Practice active listening with the constituents in the community. In this way, leaders can gain knowledge of the experiences and needs in their school community.

- When family members, caregivers, students, and staff share concerns or complaints, practice active compassionate listening and ask probing and clarifying questions. Consider not only the concern but also its root. This will allow you to take on the perspectives of others and therefore respond in ways that are empathetic and compassionate. Often people just want to be heard and validated.

- Look for ways to connect. Consider the experiences of others and reflect on your own experiences and the experiences of those in your life. This will humanize your approach in ways that will allow your constituents to connect to you.

- If you are unclear about someone's perspective or feel in opposition to their perspective, ask questions and seek to understand. This will show vulnerability that can also build trust while validating the person sharing their perspective.

Find Connections Between School and Community

Be a *servant leader*. Servant leaders see themselves as trusted protectors of the school community. Their focus is on the success and development of all members of the school community. Therefore, in seeing their role as a trusted protector, they act with the care of their community in mind. You can present yourself as a servant leader in the following ways.

- See yourself in service to the school and local community, providing the service of leadership as a caregiver of students, staff, and families.

Taking this disposition requires trust and relationship building, perspective taking, empathy, compassion, and action. This will allow your school community to see you as part of the work and engaged alongside them.

- Advocate for your community and interrupt policies and practices within and outside of the school that marginalize or harm the students, staff, and families you serve. Stand up for the rights and needs of your community. This will build trust. Your community members will feel as if you have their back.

- Actively participate in events and school initiatives. Roll up your sleeves and get involved. This will allow you to build strong relationships. When you show up, they will too.

Connect Directly With Students, Staff, Families, and Community

Students, staff, families, and community leaders should have access to the school leader. This creates connection, belonging, and trust. To help you manage these various streams of communication, try the following.

- Develop a clear system and process for two-way communication with each constituent group. A digital mode of communication in addition to verbal communication will allow you to respond in a timely manner. Be sure to delegate communication to trusted team members on urgent matters if you are unable to respond yourself, until you are able to follow up.

- Be visible, connecting with constituents daily through in-person and multimedia channels. Transparent communication also builds trust. Frequent communication and presence create a sense of security in the school community.

- Connect with the school community informally and formally through check-ins, town halls, focus groups, one-on-one meetings, video, newsletters, social media, and electronic and paper communication. These will help you find out what constituents are experiencing and allow you to document and address specific concerns and needs. It will also allow you to celebrate great things happening in the school community.

- Consult with each stakeholder group to determine their preferred mode of communication. This will reflect how you work to meet the needs of the individual as opposed to forcing them to align to your needs. It indicates flexibility.

The reproducible "Community Relationship-Building Reflection" tool at the end of the chapter (page 98) can help you reflect on your current practices regarding relationship building and then brainstorm the ways you can improve in these practices.

Words From a Principal

This spotlight on TMALS continues Dawn's story of trust from the beginning of the chapter (page 83). As mentioned, TMALS participated in a yearlong Cahn Fellowship project and chose trust as the focus of their action research problem. The project, titled "Building Staff Trust in a High Accountability Environment," was prompted by the previous year's school survey, which showed that trust was down among school staff. It ultimately led to increases in staff perceptions of trust as measured by the NYC DOE's Learning Environment Survey.

Dawn planned and led the project along with two lead teachers, Siobhan and Kerri. The school had been using a process to share and grow best practices through intervisitations. In these, peers would visit one another's classrooms to observe instruction using a protocol where they would act as critical friends, providing "glows" (recognition of areas where peers are strong) and "grows" (areas where peers could improve) in instructional practices. The goal of the project was for staff to learn how trust can impact school climate, learning communities, and student achievement.

Although there were efforts to have staff collaborate in planning for improvements in instructional practices, many staff saw critical-friend feedback as a personal attack rather than feedback to support their growth instructionally. The lack of trust didn't allow for honest conversations about what was working and not in the classroom. The idea of the leadership team was that a focus on trust would not only build relationships among staff but also cause a growth in instructional practices across the school through teacher collaboration and feedback. Because there was a lack of trust, the team decided to conduct a series of anonymous surveys and incorporate team-building activities in response to the survey data. Opportunities for dialogue increased staff trust and ownership of school operations and goals. Patterns in the survey feedback were shared transparently, along with the strategies that would be incorporated in school policy to address the feedback.

Texts used by the leadership team to design the project included the following.

- *Ken Blanchard's (2010) "Building Trust: The Critical Link to a High-Involvement, High-Energy Workplace Begins With a Common Language"*

- *Eleanor Drago-Severson's (2004)* Helping Teachers Learn: Principal Leadership for Adult Growth and Development
- *Drago-Severson's (2008) "4 Practices Serve as Pillars for Adult Learning: Learning-Oriented Leadership Offers a Promising Way to Support Growth"*
- *Drago-Severson's (2009)* Leading Adult Learning: Supporting Adult Development in Our Schools
- *Elisa MacDonald's (2011) "When Nice Won't Suffice: Honest Discourse Is Key to Shifting School Culture"*

The project timeline included the following steps over the course of a school year.

- *The leadership team shared the purpose and context of the project with all staff.*
- *The leadership team created trust survey questions for the initial survey.*
- *Teachers and support staff took the initial survey, thus providing perspectives from all roles.*
- *The leadership team reviewed the survey feedback with staff at a subsequent meeting.*
- *The leadership team incorporated a team trust-building activity series with all staff. The activity series included the following three trust-building activities.*
  - *Object toss—to begin to build trust and discuss communication among staff*
  - *Obstacle course—to build camaraderie, teamwork, and trust among staff*
  - *Tower-building group activity—to build communication, trust, and common language*
- *The leadership team conducted a follow-up survey to gather any progress on peer relationships and teaming.*
- *The leadership team analyzed the data and used their findings to plan another targeted team-building and trust-building activity series with all staff. The activities included the following.*
  - *Trust partner obstacle course—to build trust, communication, and teamwork*

- ▸ Back-to-back drawing trust activity—to build communication, clear instructions, and common language
- The leadership team facilitated a session on co-creating staff meeting norms for use at all subsequent meetings.
- Small groups of three (teachers' choice) brainstormed norms for meetings, created a gallery walk of norms and creative performance, and compiled a list of norms that the whole staff agreed on.
- The leadership team conducted a follow-up survey to gather any progress on peer relationships and teaming.
- The leadership team shared survey results and action steps to address. The team then held another team-building and trust-building activity series with all staff.
  - ▸ Partner call and response—to build trust and persistence
  - ▸ Human webs—to build communication and teamwork
- All staff had a discussion about communication based on the last survey. Staff brainstormed next steps to continue trust building the following year.

Ultimately, there was a positive impact on the communication between staff. The sharing of best practices through intervisitations had a direct impact on student achievement, school climate, and culture. By the end of year, teachers were sharing practices at a higher rate compared to previous years. Teachers openly shared fears and hopes in relation to intervisitations across grades and had honest discussions on challenges and areas of celebration in individual teacher practice. Teacher sharing during professional development with peers increased. The sharing of teacher expertise increased teacher effectiveness in instructional practices schoolwide. The positive increase in communication impacted staff and administrative working relationships.

Visit the following websites to learn more about some of the trust-building activities the TMALS team used.

- HRDQ (https://hrdqstore.com/blogs/hrdq-blog/workplace-trust-building-activities)
- Gomada (www.gomada.co/blog/trust-team-building-activities)

Co-Creation and Co-Liberation

In chapter 4 (page 67), we discussed creating a vision for racial equity. As Dawn shared in her earlier reflection, collaboration and inclusivity are key to successful leadership. Co-creation is linked to co-liberation. *Co-liberation* is the idea that freedom is collective and connected to the liberation of others. As human beings, we benefit from working in collaboration with one another. It is the notion that we are not individually free as a humanity until we are all free.

While every decision a leader makes may not be a consensus, it is important to include the school community, as much as it is possible, in any effort you want to succeed. Shifting school culture, policies, and practices that marginalize others, investigating beliefs, and practicing critical consciousness are challenging efforts. This work must happen in an environment that is trusting, caring, compassionate, and collaborative. This learning happens collectively and with support. Kara Ieva and Jordon Beasley (2022) detail a process of collaboration for educators who are striving to create culturally affirming environments to support and learn with and from one another while shifting to an asset-based approach. All members of the school community should see themselves as part of the vision. Their voices, input, needs, hopes, and desires should be reflected. In this way, there is a personal responsibility, a connection, and a commitment to the success of the vision. Success becomes a collective effort and collective celebration when achieved.

Teacher Agency

Dawn described that early in her career, she believed leadership was making decisions and sharing directives. It was only through the trusting relationship she had with her staff members, who compassionately and honestly shared challenges, that she was able to see the impact of this lack of inclusiveness on her staff. Dawn created leadership roles for her staff that empowered them to share the needed feedback for the success of the school community.

Collaboration and inclusivity are key to successful leadership.

Laurie Calvert (2016) explains that to foster professional learning for teachers, school leaders must create opportunities for teacher agency. Distributive leadership requires that leaders provide opportunity for educators to collaborate and occupy leadership roles with support. According to Calvert (2016), the learning that teachers gain through agency can occur when leaders do the following.

- Provide time for collaboration between staff members. Ensure your daily schedule allows for common planning and intervisitations.
- Consult teachers in developing professional learning plans. Conduct a survey on the areas teachers would like to grow. Where possible,

differentiate professional development to meet teachers' individual needs. Introduce teacher-supported and self-guided action research projects as a form of professional development.

- Engage teachers in analyzing data and problems of practice. Be transparent with data. Regularly ground conversations around student outcomes in the data. Engage in progress monitoring and root cause analysis, support teachers in using data to make instructional decisions, and reteach and modify lessons when needed.

- Ensure that teacher growth is at the center of all professional learning. Prioritize professional learning that is growing teacher practice and efficacy and directly connected to increased student outcomes.

Students and families are also important constituents whose sense of agency you can support. They are key constituents of the mission and vision of the school and should be engaged as active participants with voice and choice.

Student and Family Agency

As with teacher agency, student agency can advance learning and a sense of leadership and belonging. In Ladson-Billings's (1995a) foundational work, the third component of culturally relevant pedagogy is that "students must develop a critical consciousness through which they challenge the status quo of the current social order" (p. 160). Leaders and educators must create the structures and opportunities for students to develop the knowledge and skills needed to acknowledge oppression and marginalization, and then the ability to exercise agency to challenge these practices. Educational leadership scholars Katherine Cumings Mansfield, Anjalé Welton, and Mark Halx (2018) argue that providing agency through student voice allows students to engage in critical consciousness, interrogate oppressive structures, and experience healing through empowerment and collective action. Leaders can increase student agency in a number of ways, including the following.

- Create a student council. This provides an opportunity for student leadership as well as a chance for them to engage in civic leadership. You can maintain a pulse on student experiences and needs across the community.

- Ensure that students have a place at the table and can give feedback on impactful changes. This will allow students to feel confident in those leading and will also encourage them to take an active role and pride in their school community.

- Provide opportunities for students to give feedback on classroom culture and academic strategies and act on their concerns and ideas where possible. This will ensure that students' voice and experiences are included in decision making.

- Provide opportunities for student ownership in chosen community service projects and school culture initiatives. This increases positive school culture and ownership over the care of the school community.

- Seek feedback from students on how units are being taught, what is working for them, and what they would like to see in the curriculum. This will allow for student voice, choice, and increased interest in the topics being taught. They will experience a deeper connection to the learning.

Another stakeholder group in the school community that should experience agency is families. In educational settings where families are typically receivers of information and not active participants and decision makers, there is a need to empower families to join leaders and educators in analyzing, planning, and implementing school initiatives. When families are included and knowledgeable, it can also reduce resistance, as they have had opportunities throughout to have their voices heard and needs reflected in decisions made on behalf of their children. Actions such as the following increase families' sense of agency.

- Ensure your parent association is active, supported, informed, and included. Keep them in the loop, and be sure to share school data, goals, strategies, and needs. This will direct their engagement in support of the school's efforts.

- Ensure that parents and caregivers are at the table giving feedback on impactful changes. This will allow them to feel confident in your leadership and like they have an active, respected role and pride in their school community.

- Provide opportunities for parents and caregivers to give feedback on school culture, events, initiatives, and academic strategies and to act on their concerns and ideas where possible. This will ensure that families are included in decision making and play an active role.

- Seek feedback from families and caregivers on what is working for them and what they would like to see more of in your leadership. This will allow for family advocacy, inclusion, and awareness.

Conclusion

In this chapter, we examined the benefits of building school and community relationships, and the purpose and need for building relational trust. We heard about Dawn's experience with receiving honest feedback about her leadership style in relationship to inclusivity and decision making and how she engaged her teacher leaders to support change. Leaders must co-create the school's vision in collaboration with the school community through building agency and voice among teachers, students, and families. We hope that you have reflected on your current practices in building relationships and where you can become more consistent.

In the next chapter, we will investigate how leaders can be advocates for their school communities. Trusted, culturally responsive, and emotionally intelligent servant leaders understand the contexts of the lives of those they serve. When policies and practices marginalize or harm the school community, these leaders advocate for their academic, cultural, social, and emotional well-being. Caring advocate-leaders focus on equity, social justice, and school community wellness, and support the growth of the full school community. After engaging in the following reflective questions, please see the suggested "Potential Action Steps" reproducible (page 99) to help you implement these protocols in your school.

Questions for Reflection and Discussion

Please reflect on the following questions, alone or in a book discussion group, to consider the chapter content and your current and future leadership practices.

1. What new knowledge did you gain about school and community relationship building?

2. Upon reflecting on your own practices in trust and relationship building, have you made any discoveries about areas you want to address in your leadership style?

3. What barriers do you anticipate in building relationships within your school community?

4. What are your thoughts about the connections between cultural responsiveness, SEL, and relationship building?

Community Relationship-Building Reflection

Reflect on your current practices regarding community relationship building and then brainstorm ways you can improve these practices.

Community Relationship-Building Actions	My Current Practices	Actions to Improve My Practices
Engage in supportive, understanding, and positive communication with all staff, students, and families.		
Take the perspectives of others with empathy.		
Find connections between school and community.		
Connect directly with students, staff, families, and community.		

Source: Brooks DeCosta, D. (2020). Black principal perspectives on social-emotional learning and culturally responsive leadership in urban schools: The role of beliefs, values, and leadership practices *[Doctoral dissertation, Columbia University]*. Columbia Academic Commons. Accessed at https://academiccommons.columbia.edu/doi/10.7916/d8-qv6y-6846 on July 29, 2024.

The Change You Want to See © 2025 Solution Tree Press • SolutionTree.com
Visit **go.SolutionTree.com/leadership** to download this free reproducible.

Potential Action Steps

In the potential action steps for chapter 5, you have the opportunity to deepen the work and operationalize a practice or practices you and your team would like to begin with. Choose as many or as few as you are able. Consider quality over quantity and think of these possible action steps as opportunities to grow, strengthen, and build on as opposed to steps to take all at once.

- Use the "Community Relationship-Building Reflection" reproducible (page 98) to pinpoint the areas you want to focus on to build consistency.
- Conduct a survey or engage staff, students, and families in focus groups or one-on-one conversations about their perspectives on relationships among the school community members.
- Analyze the response data, share trends with the community, and engage a team that represents each of the stakeholder groups to address the feedback.
- Share the team's plan with the full school community and request more feedback.
- Develop a personal plan of action to support the continuity of this work.
- Plan to conduct survey or feedback cycles to inform school relationship culture. Empower the team to collaborate with you in designing these cycles.

Note: Remember, this work will take time. It is continuous and ongoing. Pace yourself according to the needs of your community.

6

Committing to Advocacy

This chapter explores the third component of CRASEL: serving as a caring advocate your school community. Because schools are integral parts of their communities, a school must have thorough knowledge of its surrounding community and context to respond to the needs of students and families in a culturally responsive manner. The wider community can also serve as a resource for enhancing what the school can provide. The community is something to celebrate, but there may be elements and experiences in the wider community that negatively impact students and families and their experiences in school. The school community itself must also engage in cycles of self-reflective practice, examining policies and practices that may marginalize groups of students, to make adjustments toward an asset-based approach for all students. These practices may surface in discipline policies, instructional practices, access to advanced courses, analysis of data for subgroups of students, communication with families, and more. You need to confront practices that are exclusionary, whether they come from inside or outside of the school community (Khalifa et al., 2016).

In this chapter, we will outline the ways a culturally responsive and affirming social-emotional leader advocates for their staff while creating a culture of care for students and families. The goal of this advocacy is to uplift the school community, create an emotionally safe environment, improve outcomes for students, and resist and challenge any deficit images of students and families that negatively impact the school community.

Words From a Principal

Throughout my time as principal, I've felt a natural kinship with the communities I've served. Sharing a common culture with most of the community allowed me a familiarity with the daily lives of my students, their joys, hopes, dreams, sorrows, barriers, and challenges they faced on a regular basis. During my education career, there have been occurrences in the local and wider community that caused emotional and sometimes physical distress and trauma for the members of the school. Over the years, violence, racism, brutality, school shootings, food insecurity, and neighborhood equity-based needs have been some of the issues that I've seen impact students, families, and staff. In a social and emotional approach that is culturally responsive, we do not ignore the lived experiences or traumas that affect the emotional and physical state of our community members.

While I made a concerted effort as a leader to celebrate the community, its beauty, and its cultural wealth and resources, it was also essential for me to support my community through challenges coming from outside of the school that impacted their ability to thrive emotionally, socially, and academically. I remember this most with the murder of George Floyd by a police officer during the height of the COVID-19 pandemic. We were working remotely at the time. The full school and wider community were all primarily homebound, and therefore a captive audience to the incident, which played on media repeatedly. Our students not only watched the incident, but also were home with adults and privy to conversations where even the adults had difficulty processing what was sadly a familiar scene. This time, it was captured via video in a way that was excruciating to experience physically and emotionally. As a Black woman, with a Black husband and son whom I've come to fear for daily with the level of violence against Black men, I felt retraumatized by the murder.

Although I struggled to manage the pain and trauma of the incident, I saw a need to provide the school community with a collective platform for us to share our grief and support for one another and allow us to collectively begin to process the trauma we were feeling. Because I worked in a school where our approach was culturally responsive and social-emotional, we had systems and practices in place to advocate for and support our students. It was familiar for us to engage in social justice conversations, sharing developmentally appropriate opportunities for students to express their feelings around events happening locally, nationally, and even globally that negatively impacted communities.

We had to think creatively about how to do this in a virtual setting where we worked to stay connected while being physically distanced from one another. We developed lessons for grades K–5 on loving the skin we are in, advocating for cultural holidays like Juneteenth, celebrating the contributions of people of color to U.S. history, examining and comparing activists' efforts over the years (such as the civil rights movement, Me Too, and Black Lives Matter), and writing essays and having discussions on police brutality in communities of color. One of our classes created a ten-point program advocating for change in policing. We used conversation platforms and interactive online tools such as Padlet and Flipgrid for teachers, students, parents, and grandparents to record their feelings in words or video to share with the community. It was important as a process of healing that we also gave a platform for the community to share their hopes for the future and actions they would personally take to effect a change in society. It was gripping and powerful to collectively share and work together to build awareness while supporting the healing and restoration we needed through advocacy and actions toward change.

Words From a Professor

The third tenet of CRSL (page 19) calls on leaders to establish partnerships with school communities. Though there are several reasons to do so, the hope is that by engaging in this intentional process, leaders will collaborate with the community to define educational justice for the students in their schools. By appropriately inviting input from the community, they will be undertaking a process that validates positive practices in the community. That means leaders must devise ways to get to know their community and recognize its assets.

CRSL calls on principals to engage across the entire community to learn how racial marginalization, unequal power dynamics, and oppression have affected its members. Of course, a leader should have completed our recommended exercises on racial autobiographies (page 71). Failing to complete this reflection places the principal in an awkward situation, but completing such a reflection and then seeking to support the community increases one's chances of becoming a self-aware advocate.

In considering the example Dawn shared, imagine if she had decided not to address the murder of George Floyd and the impact that it had on her community composed primarily of parents and students of color. As a Black woman leader working with Black and Brown students and their families, she would have missed an opportunity to empathize and connect, and they would have felt some degree of disappointment and perhaps even had questions about her ability as a principal to relate to their trauma. There likely would have been sincere questions about her authenticity as well.

However, because Dawn recognized the heavy emotional and psychological weight that this sad and tragic event created, she slowed down her thinking to consider the most compassionate and appropriate steps to take next. She demonstrated the strong need to be an emotionally intelligent leader who may not have had all the answers, but who showed empathy, which was needed most of all. Leaders can be great administrators and managers, but they must have compassion for their students, and have confidence in their ability to learn (Gooden, 2005; Lomotey, 1989).

Leaders who employ the CRASEL framework recognize that doing the intellectual and emotional work of grappling with identity is more than a feel-good or feel-bad exercise. It is a way for leaders to deepen their empathy and manage their emotions in ways that show vulnerability and strength, courage, and sincere concern.

RELATE AND REFLECT
- How do you relate to Dawn's experience as a leader needing to find a way to respond to community and societal issues impacting students and families?
- How have you experienced advocacy or social justice in your school community?
- What concerns do you have about bringing conversations or support structures that respond to societal concerns into your school community?
- What might you need to support your students and families this way?

Advocacy and Social Justice Leadership

In chapter 5 (page 83), we discussed the need for leaders to build trusting relationships with and within their school communities through building teacher leadership, providing opportunities for collaboration and student and staff agency, and cultivating family empowerment. We described this as a path toward co-liberation. As a further path to co-liberation, leaders co-create a compassionate, connected, and supportive community. Part of this support requires that the school be responsive to the needs of students and families through an awareness of their lived experiences. Without knowing students and families well and their sociopolitical and cultural contexts, the school is limited in its ability to appropriately respond to their needs when these issues impact their ability to thrive in school.

Khalifa and colleagues (2016), in detailing the literature on culturally responsive school leaders, emphasize the importance of advocacy and social justice leadership. They assert that this practice is "not easy given that student marginalization is often historic, normalized, and invisibilized in most educational contexts" (Khalifa et al., 2016, p. 1289). They identify that your critical self-awareness (as shared in chapter 3, page 53) is necessary for you to hold the awareness around racism and oppression or willingness to learn that will impact your ability to advocate for your students and families. Lack of such needed critical self-awareness means that you may run the risk of replicating racist structures within your school.

Culturally responsive leaders also feel a sense of urgency and need to challenge deficit mindsets and act on behalf of their students and families. David DeMatthews and Hanne Mawhinney (2014) note that social justice–oriented leaders advocate for their students with the goal of improving outcomes and conditions for students. These leaders "not only recognize inequality, but also must have the necessary competencies to take actions in ways that replace preexisting structures of inequality with more equitable structures" (DeMatthews & Mawhinney, 2014, p. 847).

The Advocate Leader

The CRASEL framework provides actions leaders can take to serve as caring advocates for all members of the school community. It's an approach to SEL that includes knowing students well and understanding their sociopolitical and cultural contexts and lived experiences to inform and guide support. The CRASEL framework, leaning on Khalifa and colleagues' (2016) literature review and CRSL framework, specifically notes "caring advocacy, challenging exclusionary practices, and valuing students' social capital" as key areas of culturally responsive school leadership and social justice advocacy (Brooks DeCosta, 2020). The CRASEL framework utilizes and expands on the social-emotional aspect of these practices (Brooks DeCosta, 2020). Serving as an advocate leader in your school community includes the following actions.

- Serve as a caring advocate and social activist for school and community.
- Resist deficit images of students and families and cultivate an asset-based approach.
- Challenge exclusionary policies and practices within and outside of school.
- Value the social capital of students.

We discuss these actions in detail in the following sections.

Serve as a Caring Advocate and Social Activist for School and Community

Earlier in this chapter, Dawn shared the ways she responded to a tragedy that was impacting the members of her school community and provided a platform for support and expression. Caring advocates are aware of what impacts the school community emotionally and physically within and outside of the school. You should seek to fully understand the community in which you work; maintain awareness of the neighborhood, resources, and challenges that persist; and know and communicate with your neighbors around the school. You should also hold an awareness of the societal concerns that impact the community you serve. And with this understanding, you can advocate for your staff, students, and families as policies, practices, and mindsets impact them.

You can advocate for teachers when communicating with families and officials, support them with compensation or time when they take on additional tasks, provide them with leadership opportunities, and advocate for funding for the resources they need.

You can advocate for students by ensuring equitable policies and practices are in place within the school community. Conduct this advocacy by analyzing data for all groups of students, frequently observing classroom teaching practices, providing feedback and opportunities for collaboration, and immediately interrupting any action, policy, or practice that marginalizes or excludes students. You can also regularly listen to and gather feedback from students on their experiences in school to make informed decisions and examine the effectiveness of policies and practices within the school.

You can advocate for families by using their influence and voice to push for needed local resources, meet with local politicians and activists to champion changes in infrastructure or resources needed in the neighborhood, meet with local precincts and community organizations to gather support and resources for families, and promote safety in the neighborhood. You can ensure there are structures in place to connect families with community resources that can support them with everyday needs.

Resist Deficit Images of Students and Families and Cultivate an Asset-Based Approach

As part of a culturally responsive approach, leaders and educators hold high expectations. They see the unlimited potential in their students and families and therefore work to support them in reaching their highest heights. When teachers believe in the abilities of the students, they teach to that ability. When leaders and teachers hold a deficit mindset, it limits their creativity and willingness to push toward growth because they do not believe it's possible. It reduces the quality of their own teaching and leadership. Engaging staff in a discussion of a research-based article or text on asset-based pedagogy and growth mindsets is a useful approach to building educator knowledge. Once the staff build their knowledge about asset-based approaches, they can engage in a self-reflective practice using an equity tool to determine where they may hold deficit views of groups of students and families.

As mentioned, a deficit mindset impacts the ways teachers teach and leaders lead and the quality of their instruction and leadership. For example, if a teacher holds a view that a student will not be able to succeed in a certain content area, they may apply too many scaffolds, curtail the student's perseverance, or limit the student's access to materials. When a teacher holds an asset-based view of the student's abilities, they challenge them, they provide multiple resources, they allow them to productively struggle, and they expect more from them. You should be a model of this self-reflective practice by transparently challenging your own beliefs and mindsets as a public learner for your staff. After giving staff the support and opportunity to build their knowledge and examine their own beliefs, you can move the staff into action through engaging in an equity audit of school policies and practices.

Here are some literary resources for building an asset-based mindset in your school community.

- "Meeting Student Trauma With an Asset-Based Approach" (Alvarez-Ortiz, Haynes, & Zacarian, 2020)
- "Looking at Data Through an Equity Lens" (Bocala & Boudett, 2022)
- "5 Elements of a Positive Classroom Environment for Students Living With Adversity" (Zacarian, Alvarez-Ortiz, & Haynes, 2018)
- "3 Steps to Developing an Asset-Based Approach to Teaching" (Lalor, 2020)

Challenge Exclusionary Policies and Practices Within and Outside of School

The equity audit process is an excellent way to engage students, staff, and families in a process of self-reflection. An equity audit analyzes and examines the school's mission, vision, and values and juxtaposes those ideals with the goals, practices, policy, and actual data for all subgroups of students within the school. In the equity audit, the team, without disclaimers or excuses, examines various forms of data such as suspensions, incidents, academic achievement, attendance, and so on to determine whether all students are receiving equitable support or whether there is a particular group or groups within the school who are not experiencing success. The team can determine what shifts are needed to ensure equity in policy and practices such as discipline, grading, instruction, support, access, and so on.

Part of the equity audit can include empathy interviews. These conversations with various constituencies within the school community gauge qualitative information on their experiences in the school, giving clarity on the multiple perspectives within the school. It is important that the process is transparent and includes representation from all constituent groups to allow for multiple perspectives. It is also imperative that when and if you find practices and policies that have marginalized or excluded students, the team collaborates to take action and adjust those practices to make them more equitable. See the National Association of Elementary School Principals' (2021) "New School Equity Audit Tool" (www.naesp.org/news/new-school-equity-audit-tool) for more information on the process. We explain empathy interviews further in the Words From a Principal section of this chapter (page 109).

Value the Social Capital of Students

Social scientists Mi Young Ahn and Howard H. Davis (2020) outline three components of social capital, including trust, social network, and participation. They note that a sense of belonging represents ease, safety, respect, and connectedness as indicators of social capital (Ahn & Davis, 2020). A student's social capital is directly linked to student agency and voice. From a leader's perspective, including student voice and leadership in this work can lead to authentic student ownership, not only for the student leader but also for their peers. This can also build authentic relationships, understanding, and belonging among peers as well as trust as they observe students at the center, supporting the leadership in this work.

You co-create the safe environment that fosters the trust that allows for emotional and physical safety, which students need to feel a sense of belonging and connectedness.

In chapter 5 (page 83), we discussed the need to build caring, supportive relationships within the school community and the ways this can happen through agency, trust, and empowerment. This connects directly with advocacy in that you create and prioritize the conditions where relationships are honored and built. You co-create the safe environment that fosters the trust that allows for emotional and physical safety, which students need to feel a sense of belonging and connectedness. Both CRSL and SEL build relationships and belonging, but this is a priority that leaders must advocate for in their schedules, in their programming, and with their budgets, as decisions are made about related resources and partnerships. This may be a challenge for leaders working in high-accountability environments. However, knowing the value of recognizing and cultivating students' social capital and the impact on student achievement and learning is key in supporting your purpose for centering positive relationship building. Khalifa and colleagues (2016) note that as the ability to value students' social capital is not common among leaders, those who are able to do this can "tap into the genius" of all students (p. 1291).

The reproducible "Advocacy Leadership Reflection" tool at the end of the chapter (page 112) can help you to reflect on your current practices regarding advocacy action and then brainstorm the ways you can improve in these practices.

Words From a Principal

TMALS participated in an equity audit (page 107) to determine whether the school's policies and practices were equitable and in alignment with our vision for racial equity (outlined in chapter 4, page 76). With the support of the NYC DOE Office of District Charter Partnerships, the leadership team and I engaged in a self-reflective equity audit, selecting components of focus using the 2018 Mid-Atlantic Equity Consortium's (MAEC) process. The MAEC tool is extensive, with checklists for determining equity in classroom environment, instructional strategies, academic placement, and student leadership. It also identifies schoolwide practices such as policy, organization, climate, staffing, assessment, professional development, standards, curriculum, classroom management, interventions, and more.

The TMALS team used the checklist to determine one area of focus at a time. The school used data to pinpoint areas where growth was needed. The leadership team shared the findings with the full team and gathered feedback. At that time, a plan of action was created to address the area of focus.

For TMALS, the area of focus centered on expectations and intervention support for students with disabilities. This group was academically challenged, but what surfaced as a root cause was a mindset of low expectations and lack of adequate supports when students were in general education settings. There was a view that students' lower academic performance should be expected due to disability and that it was solely the responsibility of the special education teacher to address student needs. I shared information in professional development on deficit mindset and low expectations, along with strategies for building a growth mindset—not only for teachers, but also for students about their own achievement and abilities.

A feedback mechanism allowed students to provide teachers feedback on how instruction was implemented and conducted with each unit of study. Students were able to express what they needed teachers to do more of or less of for them to better grasp the topic. General education teachers participated in a refresher on reading and using students' individualized education plans throughout the day to provide adequate intervention support and scaffolds for students. The leadership team, in collaboration with special education teachers, created a checklist of best practices and resources for teachers. The leadership team then began to track the progress of students with disabilities throughout the year on periodic assessments to determine where successful practices were taking place and where more instructional support for teachers was needed.

In the areas of climate and culture, the team gathered more qualitative data on how staff, students, and families were feeling about specific elements of the audit. The empathy interview process was supported by the NYC DOE Office of School Design. This process was as follows.

1. Ensure the team conducting the interviews represents the various constituent groups in the school community, including staff, students, families, caregivers, and community members.
2. Ensure that all school community constituencies are represented among interviewees.
3. Set a goal for the interviews aligned with the area of focus from the equity audit findings.
4. Set norms for the interviews and review with the team. High Tech High Graduate School of Education's (n.d.) suggested empathy interview norms include the following.
    - Seek to understand.
    - Ask once, clearly.
    - Ask questions that elicit stories and feelings. Probe with prompts such as "Tell me more" and "What was that like for you?"
5. Prepare with the leadership team for clarity prior to the interviews to norm and calibrate.
6. Create a schedule for the interviews and conduct them using recorders and transcription.
7. Examine and analyze responses with the team, looking for patterns, common themes, root causes, and so on.
8. Use the findings to inform needed changes in policies or practices that present challenges or marginalize constituents.
9. Share the findings and action plan widely.

Other tools and resources the TMALS team used for preparation and data analysis in the equity audit include the following.

- MAEC's (2021) equity audit
- Community Tool Box's (n.d.) SWOT analysis
- Cascade Team's (2023) SOAR analysis
- Kari Nelsestuen and Julie Smith's (2020) "Empathy Interviews" article
- Rebecca Powell, Susan Chambers Cantrell, Pamela K. Correll, and Victor Malo-Juvera's (2017) Culturally Responsive Instruction Observation Protocol

Conclusion

In this chapter, we examined the ways that leaders can be advocates for their students, staff, and families inside and outside of the school by resisting deficit images, obtaining the resources needed to support students and families, challenging exclusionary policies and practices, and supporting students' social capital within the school. We told about Dawn's experience and thoughts around serving her school community as a caring advocate in a trying time. Through the lens of the CRASEL framework, we examined what advocacy leadership looks like and reflected on our current practices and goals for growth in these areas. We shared the practices at TMALS in conducting an equity audit and empathy interviews as a self-reflective practice to address school policies and practices that create inequities in the school community.

In the next chapter, we will explore ways you should and can nurture through high expectations as part of maintaining a culturally responsive approach (Gay & Kirkland, 2003). Your ability to model and create a nurturing environment where everyone sees the potential of the student, recognizes their abilities and strengths from an asset-based lens, values the knowledge and contribution of the family, and works to build on students' strengths will determine the quality of instruction, social-emotional support, and learning that exists in your school. After engaging in the following reflective questions, please see the suggested "Potential Action Steps" reproducible (page 113) to help you implement these protocols in your school.

Questions for Reflection and Discussion

Please reflect on the following questions, alone or in a book discussion group, to consider the chapter content and your current and future leadership practices.

1. What new knowledge did you gain about advocacy leadership?
2. Upon reflecting on your own practices in advocating for your school community, what discoveries have you made about areas you want to address in your leadership style?
3. What barriers do you anticipate in serving as a caring advocate for your school community?
4. What do you know about the needs and concerns of your school's surrounding community?
5. Do you foster a culture of advocacy in your staff, families, and students? If so, in what ways? If not, where might you begin?

Advocacy Leadership Reflection

Reflect on your current practices regarding advocacy leadership, and then brainstorm the ways you can improve in these practices.

Advocacy Actions	My Current Practices	Actions to Improve My Practices
Serve as a caring advocate and social activist for school and community.		
Resist deficit images of students and families and encourage an asset-based approach.		
Challenge exclusionary policies and practices within and outside of the school community.		
Value the social capital of students.		

Source: Brooks DeCosta, D. (2020). Black principal perspectives on social-emotional learning and culturally responsive leadership in urban schools: The role of beliefs, values, and leadership practices [Doctoral dissertation, Columbia University]. Columbia Academic Commons. Accessed at https://academiccommons.columbia.edu/doi/10.7916/d8-qv6y-6846 on July 29, 2024.

The Change You Want to See © 2025 Solution Tree Press • SolutionTree.com
Visit **go.SolutionTree.com/leadership** to download this free reproducible.

Potential Action Steps

In the potential action steps for chapter 6, you have the opportunity to deepen the work and operationalize a practice or practices you and your team would like to begin with. Choose as many or as few as you are able. Consider quality over quantity and think of these possible action steps as opportunities to grow, strengthen, and build on as opposed to steps to take all at once.

- Use the "Advocacy Leadership Reflection" reproducible (page 112) to identify areas where you want to grow.
- Engage your team in a discussion-based article study using a research-based text on asset-based pedagogy or growth mindset to build the staff's knowledge.
- Engage the staff in an equity audit using one of the following data sets: discipline, attendance, classroom management, school climate and culture, academic achievement, special education, or multilingual learners.
- Develop a leadership team that is representative of various constituents such as teachers, students, and parents and caregivers. Support them by conducting empathy interviews, co-created by the team, designed to address an area of concern that surfaces in the equity audit.
- Analyze the data from the audit and empathy interviews and share trends with the community. Engage the leadership team that represents each of the constituent groups to address the findings.
- Share the team's plan with the full school community and request feedback.
- Co-create an action plan to support the continual monitoring of this work toward maintaining equity in school policies and practices.

Note: Remember, this work will take time. It is continuous and ongoing. Pace yourself according to the needs of your community.

7

Nurturing Through High Expectations and Being Culturally Responsive

In this chapter, we will explore the next two elements of the CRASEL framework: nurturing through high expectations and being a culturally responsive school leader. We will share the ways you can create compassionate cultures of care while holding high expectations for all. Through a process of professional development for educators that includes using research-based instructional practices, analyzing student data, engaging in article studies featuring best practices, and enlisting quality professional development where needed, leaders can support strong instructional practices that hold high expectations for educators and students.

In a nurturing culture of high expectations, students should feel a level of care from the school community and the safety that allows them to express themselves and fulfill their potential. You can co-create an environment that cultivates and supports student voice, honors and recognizes the value of student agency, and engages students' highest capabilities. In an environment where students feel safe to make mistakes and be human, staff can approach student behavior challenges with a restorative process rather than a punitive one. This will create a compassionate, caring culture centered in understanding, restoration, and healing.

Words From a Principal

One of the joys I had as a school leader was witnessing the leadership and brilliance in my students. I learned early on that including them as leaders in school initiatives was a powerful way to build opportunities for student voice. Additionally, this student leadership seemed to build confidence, ownership, positive relationships with peers, and a sense of belonging in the school culture. This sense of confidence along with the trust we as adults had in their leadership often transferred into confidence in their studies. Even when students experienced challenges in their academics, they felt a level of acceptance and belonging that allowed them to approach challenges with self-care and self-awareness. The grace that educators offer to students in their struggles can transfer into the grace students show themselves when they face challenges. This educator's compassion was something I learned from Ms. R, as I shared in an earlier chapter (page 32).

Soon after we started using the RULER approach (page 24) across the school, I attended a mindfulness leadership retreat (which I did throughout my career and continue to do as a way to restore and rejuvenate). We were in small groups designing ways to build mindful practices in our schools. Through the collective wisdom of the small group, we came up with a plan to advance students' ownership over SEL and mindful practice through student leadership. We designed a process for a group of student leaders who would be nurtured and supported to serve as "self-awareness leaders." They would be trained to lead guided meditation and Mood Meter check-ins in the classroom. Each class from grades 1 through 5 would have at least two student self-awareness leaders. This ownership of the practices would allow self-awareness leaders agency and active participation, and they would serve as a model to their peers. In many cases, students who most needed the practices themselves for emotional regulation were chosen for these leadership roles. The level of high expectation we had for them and the weight of responsibility they held carried over into their own ability to regulate as models of leadership for their peers.

Nurturing students, even those who struggled, to a high expectation was a strategy that worked. Students pushed themselves, self-regulated, and self-corrected to continue to serve in these leadership roles. Soon, many more students wanted to serve in these roles. We created mentorships and apprenticeships between older and younger student leaders. The self-awareness leaders took on additional responsibilities, such as giving tours to guests; sharing the instructional, CRSE, and SEL practices in the school; serving as peer mediators; and more. Students observing their peers operating in leadership roles were inspired and driven to their own leadership. The belief we held in our students' potential and the high expectations we exhibited motivated them to strive to be their best selves. And even if they struggled at times, as we all do, they knew what was expected of them, they knew we cared and believed in them, and they were self-motivated to do better and to be their best. At the end of the day, they felt cared for, nurtured, trusted, and accepted. They became models for all students, and, therefore, their experiences soon became the experiences of the full school community. High expectations for all.

Words From a Professor

"Do students have First Amendment rights in schools?" I asked a group of leaders who occupied various roles within the school building. Some looked confused and frozen by what most certainly was a trick question. Others verbally confirmed, "Yes!" Still, a few exclaimed, "No, don't think so."

I often ask this question as an introduction to the idea of student leaders exercising their free speech rights and how leaders of all types feel about it. Asking "Who controls the educational process?" is another way for leaders to examine how comfortable they are opening up the educational space for student leaders and their contributions. Beyond the "correct response" to the preceding question, leaders must be clear about their position on allowing students to voice their opinions and provide input on how the educational environment is supporting them emotionally and academically.

Another reason I often start this inquiry in this way is that I would like leaders to go above and beyond what they are legally required to do on behalf of their students. CRSL encourages leaders to create a welcoming and inclusive environment that questions historical and existing barriers to one's education. As they become more aware of their own challenges and capabilities, leaders should remember this tenet of CRSL, especially as outside forces question education's role in preparing students to be educated citizens. Doing so as they consider policies and practices can help leaders better show up for students in ways that could even challenge unjust laws or policies that sometimes end up being heavily biased against Black and Brown students, who are often oversurveilled.

For example, at the time of this writing, an African American student received an in-school suspension for wearing his hairstyle in locks, a style worn by several of the men in his family for generations. His suspension went forward even as the state of Texas was adopting a version of the CROWN Act, which is an acronym for "Creating a Respectful and Open World for Natural Hair." The purpose of the law is to prohibit race-based hair discrimination, and it bars school officials from penalizing Black people who choose to show their natural hair texture or wear "protective hairstyles including Afros, braids, dreadlocks, twists or Bantu knots" (Creating a Respectful and Open World for Natural Hair Act, 2022).

Even though Texas is one of twenty-four states that has enacted a version of the CROWN Act, one school district still created and applied an unjust policy that suspended a student for wearing locks. Leaders must show up for students and define clear expectations of how they will challenge unjust policies like this.

Additionally, questioning unjust policies and their uneven application is another way to bolster students' confidence and for leaders to show the relevance of becoming more educated about a history of injustices. Encouraging students to learn their rights and providing protection for them in the process confirms that school is a place that values students and what they contribute to the educational environment, even as they are learning difficult or controversial content. Such culturally affirming behavior by leaders will give students a sense that regardless of sad, disconcerting, and unsettling events in the world, students will know that there are adults who will protect them and hold high expectations for them as members of the school community. This affirming approach of nurturing students is one of building community with and for young leaners to prosper and seek to do their best learning, which ultimately can lead to positive change.

RELATE AND REFLECT

- How do you think the student self-awareness leaders felt about Dawn and the educators who supported them and provided these roles for them?
- How do you provide opportunities for students to actively serve in a leadership role in your school community?
- How can high expectations impact students outside of their leadership responsibilities?
- Do you believe in the full potential of the students you serve? In what ways do you show you hold all students to high expectations?

The Importance of High Expectations

Cultural responsiveness, as we explained in previous chapters looking at the work of scholars such as Gay (2010) and Ladson-Billings (1995a, 1995b), includes holding students to high expectations. There is a level of trust and care that is needed to build caring, supportive relationships with students. Students who know and feel that educators and leaders care for them and want to see them succeed will apply themselves even in areas of challenge.

Walker and Snarey (2004) maintain that "care means liberating others from their state of need and actively promoting their welfare" (p. 4). This again reflects the concept of co-liberation. As Vanessa Siddle Walker's work asserts, there is much to be learned from Black educators prior to *Brown v. Board of Education* (1954) about the care and high expectations they showed students in the midst of oppression. Adah Ward Randolph and Dwan V. Robinson (2019) note that Black teachers and school leaders before *Brown v. Board* "employed a cadre of overeducated Black professionals who actively sought to be shepherds of the Black community establishing an unintended benefit of high expectations and achievement" (p. 1425). Serving as role models, the highly qualified educators saw unlimited potential in their students and expected excellence from them.

Kofi Lomotey and Kendra Lowery (2014) find that Black principals who hold high expectations, center students' needs, and believe that students need more than academic success experience success in their leadership. Like the educators before *Brown v. Board*, these school leaders focus on the whole child, nurturing their students and serving as role models for those who need them (Lomotey & Lowery, 2014). Aligned to those findings, Pontso Moorosi, Kay Fuller, and Elizabeth Reilly (2018) emphasize how Black female principals are "pupil-centered" and focus on their students' "holistic development" (p. 154). The idea of care is central to SEL. The caring aspect of SEL aligns with a culturally responsive approach. We would argue that the two approaches should be employed simultaneously as a fully holistic approach to student learning and support, and the CRASEL framework provides ways to enact them.

Valuing the approach of Black educators who supported students during highly traumatic times provides us invaluable strategies. These educators exhibited deep care and high expectations for their students while they were also suffering. In her seminal research, Linda C. Tillman (2008) celebrates the work of educator Asa Hilliard and his study of the Zion School's culturally responsive approach. Tillman (2008) asserts that Black school leaders before *Brown v. Board:*

> exhibited various forms of caring: exposing students to good teachers and good teaching, being sympathetic and empathetic, being compassionate, and seeing children who were often held hostage to inequitable systems and institutional racism as human beings. These Black principals were master leaders, gap-closers, innovators, translators and transformers. They exhibited what Dr. Hilliard argued that all students must have beyond tests or alternative teaching techniques, "love." (p. 602)

Muhammad (2020), whose work is widely used in classrooms across the United States, encourages educators to see the genius in their students. This grounds high expectations and belief in the full potential of all students.

A Safe and Nurturing Environment

The CRASEL framework describes nurturing through high expectations as featuring the following strategies.

- Create a safe environment for all learners.
- Engage student voice.
- Enact positive discipline practices.
- Use data to inform students' instructional needs.
- Ensure academics are rigorous, project based, and challenging for diverse learners.
- Curate and provide high-quality professional development.

We discuss these strategies in detail in the following sections.

Create a Safe Environment for All Learners

Creating a safe environment for all learners starts with you. The expectations for how educators interact with students and cultivate classroom cultures and how students interact with and relate to one another should be modeled, monitored, and nurtured by you. Leaders and school systems often have discipline codes and regulations about the physical safety of students and consequences for violating those codes and regulations. Be sure to follow these regulations so as not to violate the rights of students and staff in the school community. However, incidents such as bullying that compromise students' feeling of safety originate in relationships and emotional regulation. Here are some possible action steps you can take to foster a safe school environment.

- In collaboration with your community, co-create the expectations and norms for a safe school culture. Collaborating either with your staff, parent association, or school leadership team and student government includes more perspectives and voices while creating norms. This will increase ownership in the school norms and expectations among all constituencies.
- Be sure to include families in the creation of these expectations. Through a survey or focus group, allow families and caregivers decision-making input about norms and expectations and communicate widely that this is a co-created process. Including families in the process may mitigate pushback against the school's chosen expectations.
- Co-create a set of expectations around how members of the school community should interact to maintain physical safety.

Communicate the expectations widely and celebrate successes. This will allow you to hold clear expectations for behavior while also fostering positive relationships in classrooms and schoolwide.

- Use student feedback to continually gauge whether the environment is physically and emotionally safe. Address concerns directly, take action, and communicate expectations widely. Use your discipline code to hold all members of the school community accountable for everyone's physical and emotional safety. Ensure that all constituencies know the school's discipline code and any related consequences. Ensure there are opportunities for restorative justice circles for healing relationships and positively reintegrating students to the school community.

- Ensure that in addition to students' physical and emotional safety, they are also safe to make mistakes, to be vulnerable, to express themselves, and to share difficulties with a trusted adult. This safety in the classroom can allow students a space to be themselves and to thrive in a caring community. Teachers are key in the caring community cultures that they cultivate in and among their students.

Engage Student Voice

We described earlier in the chapter the need to create leadership opportunities and engage student voice as a form of high expectations for students. The Yale RULER (see page 24) approach engages students in creating a charter that serves as an agreement between all members of the classroom community. A charter can be an important tool. It addresses how students want to feel as a community, what they will do to feel those feelings as a community, and how they will address conflicts that arise. Students should be active participants in the creation of the charter; their voices are central with the teacher as a facilitator, contributor, and guide. Everyone in the community signs the charter agreement. Keep the following in mind when creating a charter.

- An ideal charter replaces a list of "do not" rules with an asset-based perspective that tells what the community *does* want to feel and experience.

- A charter is always in draft form. It is a working document that students and staff check in on regularly to determine where they are successful and where more attention is needed. As issues arise, students and staff can revise the charter to support the healthiest environment in the classroom. This is an example of a process that fully engages student voice.

- Students are active participants and creators of expectations, not just receivers. Students are facilitators of the expectations and norms in the classroom. This allows for internalization and ownership of positive interactions in and beyond the classroom.

Allowing students to provide teachers and leaders feedback through surveys and focus groups also engages their voice in school decision making.

Enact Positive Discipline Practices

Once schools and classrooms have expectations about how they will treat one another and environments are physically and emotionally safe, schools still need systems to address any harm that occurs in the school community. Naturally, student conflict and challenges will surface within the school, resulting from things such as students interactions, personal crises, or home-life challenges. Psychologists Stephanie Little and Rachel E. Maunder (2021) note that trauma can impact how students interact with teachers, staff, and peers. It is important to maintain a safe environment and hold everyone accountable to how they treat one another while handling incidents that violate the school's discipline code in restorative ways. The following are examples of actions you can take to ensure positive discipline practices.

It is important to maintain a safe environment and hold everyone accountable to how they treat one another while handling incidents that violate the school's discipline code in restorative ways.

- Hold students accountable for their behavior, especially in instances where there is harm, and at the same time offer those students an opportunity for restoration, forgiveness, and re-entry into the classroom. This can help them re-engage with their peers, understand the impact of their actions, and, along with ongoing support, increase their ability to self-regulate moving forward.
- Use tools such as restorative circles, healing circles, Meta-Moments, serenity spaces, and peer mediation that support a restorative discipline approach. This will allow students who have been removed or suspended to reintegrate into the school community through a relationship-healing approach, with the goal of eliminating further harm.

Use Data to Inform Students' Instructional Needs

Data-driven decision making can help target support for students to their individual needs, whether those needs are for intervention or advancement. Reviewing the data as discussed in chapter 6 (page 101) can also indicate whether all students are receiving what they need in an equitable manner. High expectations require educators to provide students with what they need individually to succeed. Educators can do this in various ways, such as the following.

- Analyze data in cycles throughout the school community using various forms of data, including academic, assessment, attendance, student work, student surveys, teacher surveys, parent surveys, and so on. This allows for a more complete picture of what is happening using multiple data sets providing a holistic picture of needs and successes.

- Use quantitative and qualitative data for a fuller picture of the needs of students and individual subgroups of students. The qualitative data may provide information that the quantitative data do not.

- Engage teachers in teamwork to collect, analyze, and utilize data to make informed decisions and show that they have support of school leadership. Provide time for such teamwork. Communicate that analyzing data is a priority and provide adequate time and support to engage in this important work.

- Set up flexible grouping in classrooms, allowing modifications to curriculum, intervention supports, scaffolding of instructional tasks, and more. This can address student needs that show up as root causes in student data.

- Include students in reviewing their own data. It is also important for older students to be aware of their data as information, including where they are most successful and where they may want to apply themselves further.

Using data should always come from an asset-based approach, looking not only for areas of need but also for areas of strength to build on in student learning. Knowing students well, including their successes, interests, and challenges, will allow educators to design instruction that maximizes learning and meets their needs.

Ensure Academics Are Rigorous, Project Based, and Challenging for Diverse Learners

In encouraging an academic program that reimagines the way we teach to the full potential of all students, we encourage the use of Gholdy Muhammad's historically responsive literacy (HRL) model. In Muhammad's (2020) *Cultivating Genius*, she details her HRL model as an equity model that asserts a curriculum and lesson design valuing and centering the lives and experiences of all students, including Black and Brown students, in their everyday learning. When the curriculum is representative of all students, including the most marginalized, there is an equitable approach to learning. The four layers of the HRL model include identity, skills, criticality, and intellectualism (Muhammad, 2020).

1. Identity is "composed of notions of who we are, who others say we are and whom we desire to be" (Muhammad, 2020, p. 67).

2. Skills and proficiencies are defined as "denoting competence, ability, and expertise" as they relate to the area of study (Muhammad, 2020, p. 85).

3. Criticality "helps teachers understand and explain inequities in education and is a step towards anti-oppression" (Muhammad, 2020, p. 117).

4. Intellectualism is "what we learn or understand about various topics, concepts, and paradigms" (Muhammad, 2020, p. 104).

This approach to lesson design cultivates students' excellence and genius and holds high expectations for all students, including diverse learners. The learning is not only representative of the students' culture and the culture of others, but is also multifaceted, using multiple literacies including spoken language, varied texts, art, and music, which encourages a project-based, real-world-connected approach to learning that is rigorous, relevant, responsive, and engaging, providing entry for diverse learners.

Curate and Provide High-Quality Professional Development

Just as learning should be rigorous for students and representative of high expectations, so should be the learning opportunities for educators and support staff. There are various learning opportunities for school staff. In the traditional sense, professional development in specific curriculum areas prepares staff for the effective implementation of specific curriculum content. Connecting with and curating high-quality professional development takes time and research. Often there is also expertise within the school or at nearby schools where intervisitation and teacher-led professional development can be highly beneficial.

Creating a culture of intervisitation, which can happen once trust is built, includes teacher peers providing critical feedback to one another, celebrating areas of strength, and providing suggestions for improvement in areas of challenge. This can create a culture of collaborative learning, which includes collaborative learning spaces where teachers can be celebrated and where they can be public learners in support of one another, ultimately leading to the collective growth of all. Creating lab classrooms in areas of teacher success and strength can also provide ongoing opportunities for capacity building and mentorship within the building for current and newly onboarded educators. For the purposes of sustainability, leveraging the expertise that exists within the building for cultivating teacher learning, leadership, and growth is a best practice. This approach also lends itself to a positive culture of lifelong learning among the staff and a community of learners.

The reproducible "Nurturing Through High Expectations Reflection" tool at the end of the chapter (page 130) can help you reflect on your current practices regarding nurturing through high expectation actions and then brainstorm the ways you can improve in these practices.

Culturally Responsive Practices

We explored CRSL in previous chapters when we discussed performing racial identity work with the school community, conducting equity audits, using data to inform the targeted needs of all subgroups of students, creating the vision for racial equity, and integrating culturally responsive texts and resources into the curriculum. A few additional key points of culturally responsive school leaders include supporting their staff in becoming more culturally responsive, modeling by the school leader, and modeling of culturally responsive practices throughout the school environment.

Your hiring and professional development practices are paramount to the success of the work. As it is imperative for students to see diversity in classroom teachers and support staff, those same staff members need ongoing support and development in equity-based, culturally responsive approaches aligned with social-emotional approaches. You should curate professional development experiences (which should be ongoing) using vetted experts. University partnerships are also useful in ensuring that educators remain abreast of current research and best practices.

As mentioned earlier, there is much to be learned from Black educators before *Brown v. Board of Education* and beyond, particularly those who led in marginalized communities. The approach of these effective leaders was as the caring advocate. Connecting with families and including them as active partners in their children's education, in whatever form they can participate, are vital. Muhammad Khalifa (2012), in his description of principal as community leader, notes that "a strong relationship between students' school and home environments was one of the most valuable assets utilized by early Black school leaders in segregated communities" (p. 425). Khalifa (2012) connects the school leader exhibiting a caring community presence to culturally responsive leadership practices.

This research further solidifies the connection and need to combine SEL with CRSL for highly effective leadership.

The following are actions you can take to engage in culturally responsive and sustaining school leadership. Start with one component at a time, then engage thoroughly before moving onto another component. Build on your school's practices slowly and with intention. Share successes widely. Quality over quantity!

- **Develop culturally responsive staff:** Serve as lead learner in the professional development of your staff in cultural responsiveness. Begin with racial reflection, autobiography sharing, and self-awareness practice. Engage in article studies with a protocol for discussion. Include the work of scholars such as Geneva Gay, Mark A. Gooden, Zaretta Hammond, Muhammad Khalifa, Gloria Ladson-Billings, Rosa Rivera-McCutchen, Gholdy Muhammad, Django Paris, and Linda Tillman. Highlight the impact of culturally responsive pedagogy on advancing student learning and engagement. Work to build their repertoire in the research on CRSE. Document the staff's collective knowledge to use later.

- **Use data to determine student needs and areas of unfinished learning:** Through your chosen equity audit tool (see page 107), conduct an audit with your team including varied constituents for

> Connecting with families and including them as active partners in their children's education, in whatever form they can participate, are vital.

multiple perspectives. Identify areas of success and areas of need in granular terms. Choose the highest-leverage areas to tackle first. Work with your team to develop an action plan differentiated for student needs. Communicate trends in the data, goals, successes, and needs widely across the school community, including families, partners, and caregivers. This work should be a collective community effort.

- **Model culturally responsive practices throughout the school day and in all spaces of the school:** Use the CRSE article research discussion data to co-create a list of non-negotiable schoolwide expectations for CRSE across all classrooms and learning spaces. Determine these non-negotiables in collaboration with staff, parents, and students. Start with five to ten expectations, and share them widely. Provide time for teachers to collaborate and integrate. Conduct supportive walkthroughs the first year to build a strong foundation. Create a model classroom or lab site to use for intervisitations, learning, and onboarding new staff. If feasible, create model teacher videos of your non-negotiable practices to use as reference and professional learning.

- **Incorporate identity and perspectives of the marginalized in the curriculum:** Work with your team to review the current curriculum. Determine where there are opportunities to ensure diverse identities and perspectives are evident in the texts and topics being taught daily. Document this in your curriculum maps and pacing guides. Engage staff and families in a book study using Muhammad's *Unearthing Joy* (2023) or *Cultivating Genius* (2020). Explore her HRL framework and provide opportunities for teachers to integrate its components in existing lessons. Develop a lab site for this work as well. Ensure all teachers have a classroom library that reflects all identities present in the classroom and at least one that is not present in the community.

- **Develop a schoolwide vision for racial equity:** Construct a team of varied constituents for multiple perspectives and voices. Analyze the equity audit findings as well as information from empathy interviews (see page 107 for resources). Co-create the vision and share widely. Regularly share the vision with loving accountability and ask the community for input on whether the school is following its vision and where there is room for growth. The vision for racial equity should serve as a guide for developing policies and practices. See page 74 for more on this process.

Words From a Principal

Graduates of TMALS often recall the leadership opportunities they experienced and how those experiences impacted them in their educational careers and further in life, regarding confidence, access, and opportunity. One of those leadership opportunities at TMALS, as Dawn mentioned earlier in this chapter, is students serving as self-awareness leaders. This section provides more detail about how to implement this process.

The idea was created to take the school's SEL and mindfulness practice to a deeper level while building more student ownership in the practices. While staff were using the practices consistently in classrooms, they found that in other spaces of the school, students were not using the practices and strategies without teacher direction. The result was disruption and conflict, specifically outside of the classroom in self-directed social spaces like breakfast, lunch, snack time, and recess.

Teachers and peers nominated student self-awareness leaders based on their self- and social awareness and interest in supporting their classroom community in social-emotional practice. Once students were selected, they were supported consistently in their roles and responsibilities. The following were the various responsibilities for student self-awareness leaders.

- *Lead a guided meditation each day at teacher-identified times.*
- *Lead the RULER Mood Meter check-in, Charter check-in, and yoga refocusing movements at teacher-identified times.*
- *Conduct tours for schools and individuals on emotional intelligence learning walks at TMALS.*
- *Meet with administration monthly and as needed.*
- *Optional: identify themselves as self-awareness leaders to the rest of the school, for example, by wearing blue shirts on Fridays.*
- *Optional: mediate small conflicts between students using the RULER Blueprint.*

Students received modeling and training in yoga brain breaks with Pure Edge online tutorials, professional development in guided meditation, and peer mediation using the RULER Blueprint.

In addition to students who were highly self-aware with a strong ability to self-regulate, TMALS gave opportunities to students who used and appreciated the practices because of their own challenges to serve as self-awareness leaders. As mentioned earlier in the chapter, students who experienced regular challenges with their own emotional regulation improved their abilities through the leadership opportunity. They not only supported their own growth, but also were able to support the growth of their peers. This practice of creating student leadership and ownership in SEL proved to be a catalyst for establishing the work as a consistent schoolwide approach and culture.

Conclusion

In this chapter, we explored how you can create a compassionate culture of care while holding high expectations for all. We explained the purpose and impact of creating these positive school cultures and the impact on the community. Dawn shared her experiences with building student agency, voice, and leadership and the positive results of that work. Mark shared how leaders can and should advocate for students to ensure equity and justice in their school experiences, interrupting and challenging policies and practices that marginalize them. We related and reflected on serving as a caring advocate with high expectations, examining our own practices in creating and supporting student leadership.

In the next chapter, we will learn more about the importance of building a positive school culture and maximizing your invaluable partnerships. We will then pull all the pieces together and examine the qualities of the culturally responsive school leader. After engaging in the following reflective questions, please see the suggested "Potential Action Steps" reproducible (page 131) to help you implement these protocols in your school.

Questions for Reflection and Discussion

Please reflect on the following questions, alone or in a book discussion group, to consider the chapter content and your current and future leadership practices.

1. What new knowledge did you gain about nurturing through high expectations?

2. Upon reflecting on your own practices in holding high expectations for students and educators, have you made any discoveries about areas you want to address in your leadership style?

3. What barriers do you anticipate in serving as a model of high expectations for your school community?

4. What area of CRSL do you feel you are successful in as a school leader? What evidence can you point to that displays your CRSL?

Nurturing Through High Expectations Reflection

Reflect on your current practices regarding nurturing through high expectations and then brainstorm the ways you can improve in these practices.

Nurturing Through High Expectations Actions	My Current Practices	Actions to Improve My Practices
Create a safe environment for all learners.		
Engage student voice.		
Enact positive discipline practices.		
Use data to inform students' instructional needs.		
Ensure an academic program that is rigorous, project based, and challenging for diverse learners.		
Curate and provide high-quality professional development for staff.		

Source: Brooks DeCosta, D. (2020). Black principal perspectives on social-emotional learning and culturally responsive leadership in urban schools: The role of beliefs, values, and leadership practices *[Doctoral dissertation, Columbia University]*. Columbia Academic Commons. Accessed at https://academiccommons.columbia.edu/doi/10.7916/d8-qv6y-6846 on July 29, 2024.

Potential Action Steps

In the potential action steps for chapter 7, you have the opportunity to deepen the work and operationalize a practice or practices you and your team would like to begin with. Choose as many or as few as you are able. Consider quality over quantity and think of these possible action steps as opportunities to grow, strengthen, and build on as opposed to steps to take all at once.

- Use the "Nurturing Through High Expectations Reflection" reproducible (page 130) to identify areas where you want to grow.
- Engage your team in a discussion-based article study using a research-based text on cultural responsiveness and high expectations to build their knowledge.
- Brainstorm with staff possible opportunities for student voice, student leadership, and student agency.
- Brainstorm with staff and students a list of the practices your school encourages that set high expectations for students and educators. Determine whether there are areas that need more development.
- Co-create an action plan to support nurturing with high expectations in your school community. If there are practices in place, determine with educators and students how to enhance them.

Note: Remember, this work will take time. It is continuous and ongoing. Pace yourself according to the needs of your community.

8

Building and Sustaining School Culture and Maximizing Partnerships

In this chapter, we will explore the final two elements of the CRASEL framework: building and sustaining school culture and maximizing partnerships. These two strategies allow leaders to infuse their approach across the school community. We will conclude by pulling together all the aspects of the CRASEL framework. After exploring several of these qualities and strategies in previous chapters, you will have the opportunity in this chapter to reflect across the areas and determine where you might grow. You will also identify next steps you can commit to growing in. Being an effective leader requires lifelong learning and the ability to adapt to the changing needs of the school community. This work is ongoing and constantly changing as we evolve as leaders.

Words From a Principal

Over the course of my eleven years as a principal, I was continually growing and adapting. During my first year, the need for social-emotional supports across my school became evident. It took some time to find the tools and practices to best support my own learning and to implement the work schoolwide. It was important, as I learned over the years, that my leadership become increasingly collaborative if I wanted to thrive and survive. This was a lesson I learned through some difficulty, but a lesson that was highly beneficial in the long run. Although my school was built on the premise of cultural responsiveness (though we didn't know the term at the time), we still lacked a cohesive approach to that work. Every classroom was like a different school, and we operated in silos. It was paramount that we co-create a vision of what SEL and cultural responsiveness would look like across classrooms and across the school. The collaboration allowed for a collective ownership of the work that did not rest with me alone.

I often tell the story of a town hall meeting I held with the students every morning at breakfast. Prior to this whole-school morning meeting, the mornings were loud, sometimes chaotic, and students would take that tone into the classroom. Teachers would have to spend valuable instructional time calming students down from whatever happened at breakfast and mediating conflicts, which could impact the rest of the day. I had over two hundred K–5 students. I realized that we needed to shift the way we started our days. I hoped that setting a positive tone at the start of the day would positively impact the remainder of the day. It was my opportunity to actively engage in the work I was expecting of my teachers; it allowed me to connect personally with my students and to be a model of the practices.

At the morning meeting, I played music for the students as they entered. I had our student self-awareness leaders assist me with the entry. Two student greeters were at the door saying "Good morning" to all who entered. Quiet music played during breakfast while students ate and then read quietly. When the teachers arrived to pick up the students, we had a ten-minute routine that included singing "Lift Every Voice and Sing," a supportive Mood Meter check-in with a few students sharing aloud, a whole-school recitation of selected poems we learned together (including "Dreams" by Langston Hughes, "Caged Bird" by Maya Angelou, "We Wear the Mask" by Paul Laurence Dunbar, and many more), and finally a whole-school guided meditation. I maintained this practice for all my years as principal. I arrived early enough to set up, get the music going before the students arrived, and distribute books to tables for quiet reading.

As the years went on, I received more help from others. In terms of being committed and consistent, I made sure I led this practice daily without fail in the beginning. It wasn't until about year three of doing this alone that I happened to come in late one morning and, for the first time, walked in and heard the music playing without me. It was then that I knew that my efforts were not in vain—the practice had become a staple and an expectation of the community. A schoolwide practice. The time, dedication, consistency, and commitment from me as the leader were key to the successful implementation of this schoolwide practice that ensured a calm, positive start to the school day.

Words From a Professor

Building and sustaining school culture are important components of CRASEL that represent aspirational points for leaders. What should leaders implement when they would like their school environment to embrace a caring culture? When it comes to developing a vision, the work of leaders is not always discernible or clearly outlined. Therefore, leaders must be committed to embedding routines that show how aspects of CRASEL are part of the culture. While doing so does not replace a vision, it provides guidance and support for the work required to build a caring school. Consistently proposing and executing relevant routines will ultimately develop what I call rhythms of leadership. In this sense, I think of rhythm *(n.d.) as it's defined by Merriam-Webster: "movement, fluctuation, or variation marked by the regular recurrence or natural flow of related elements." Those routines are the tasks that leaders and staff complete in support of a culturally responsive and caring environment. The rhythm is the binding connection between those tasks and affirming practices that support all in the emotionally affirming and developing space that becomes the school.*

By continuing to center relationships as the driving force behind this emotionally centered and supportive work, leaders and their staff create spaces to engage in and promote self-awareness, self-care, and self-management. While demonstrating each of these qualities is important for the principal, it is also crucial to integrate opportunities to allow others time to reflect on their self-awareness and how it supports their emotional well-being. Ultimately, when leaders (including teachers and staff) are more self-aware, they can practice self-care by leaning on others when needed. They can also participate more fully as part of learning communities committed to the same goals. Considering the story from earlier, when Dawn was unable to start the meditation session, another leader stepped in because the routine was a part of an important rhythm that called on those in relationship with her and the work to do something. It serves as a powerful indicator of the need to sustain the emotionally centered goals of the school's work.

Leaders have points of growth and self-management that must be part of pushing the work forward and beyond themselves. For instance, how can principals relate effectively to a range of staff personalities unless they are constantly considering aspects of self-management? How committed are school leaders to the work when it becomes extremely difficult to maintain emotional stability or when there is a lack of support for ideas and perhaps even their vision, which we hope is collectively created? How might leaders manage their emotions in ways that support others even as they resist positive change to inequitable systems and refuse to add their support before learning more? School and community relationship building becomes a goal of this process as it sets the foundation for advocacy for students and the larger community as promoted by the leaders.

> **RELATE AND REFLECT**
> - What do you think of the consistent approach Dawn took on her own for the first three years of her morning meeting?
> - Can you identify the culturally responsive and social-emotional aspects of Dawn's morning meeting with the school community?
> - How might you create an experience at the start of the day that would be culturally responsive to your school community and address its social-emotional needs? What would be your desired impact?

School Culture

Gay (2010), as one of the pioneers of CRSE, asserts that the responsibility for cultural responsiveness does not rest with the teacher and curriculum alone. School leaders must also exhibit the qualities of CRSE schoolwide as part of the school's full climate and culture. As we've discussed, construction of the vision for racial equity, discipline policy, curriculum design, and so on should be approached with collaboration and co-creation. This theme of distributive leadership extends not only to teachers and support staff who need to own the practices but also to students and parents through leadership opportunities, agency, and voice.

It is also essential to make the expectations for CRASEL tangible and clear to all members of the school community. What should these practices look, sound, and feel like in your school community? What are the specific daily practices that leaders, students, staff, and families will engage in and experience in CRASEL? The list of non-negotiables around these expectations should be co-created. Consider Dawn's daily morning practice as a ritual and routine. In her Ready for Rigor framework, which directly informs the CRASEL framework, Hammond (2015) details a robust list of culturally responsive expectations, rituals, routines, and tangible practices directly connected to cognitive learning that can be implemented in classrooms and schoolwide. In collaborative learning communities, you serve as a lead learner to model and build positive school culture.

We have also discussed feedback cycles from the school community as a distributive leadership practice to engage the voice of the school community. School culture—which should be a data point, as mentioned in the equity audit process (page 107)—should be continually assessed through quantitative data such as incident, attendance, suspension, and school climate surveys but also through qualitative means such as open-ended surveys, focus groups, and empathy interviews. The qualitative data gathered in feedback cycles can continually inform the daily experiences in the school community and allow you to address areas that may not clearly surface in quantitative data, such as microaggressions, disparities, bullying, and feelings of isolation in the school community. And finally, as Dawn shared in chapter 3 (page 53) with her experience modeling racial identity work with her staff, vulnerability and transparency can create connection and build relationships between you and the community you serve.

The following list details what building and sustaining school culture looks like in CRASEL leadership.

- **Co-create the school's mission and vision with the school community:** Once you have built the understanding and knowledge of your staff and school community in SEL and CRSL and have spent time exploring and engaging in both schoolwide, revisit your mission and vision and collectively revise as needed with a team that represents all constituencies. Share the newly co-created mission and vision and gather feedback from the full community through a survey. Adjust as needed. Publish the mission and vision and share regularly and widely to ensure everyone's awareness.

- **Clearly articulate expectations of co-created, research-based, tangible aspects and non-negotiables in CRASEL across the school community:** Revisit the CRSE non-negotiables and include the SEL non-negotiables on one CRASEL checklist of things to look for. Do this in collaboration with the constituent group that created the mission and vision. Share the draft with the full community for feedback and make adjustments as needed. Communicate the expectations widely. Create a lab classroom and resource list for teachers. Provide time for teachers to plan and conduct intervisitations. Conduct supportive walkthroughs with your constituent group and provide glows and grows for teachers with an asset-based lens.

- **Align co-created practices, rituals, and routines inside and outside of classrooms schoolwide:** Ensure that along with the expectations and non-negotiables in classrooms students can experience CRASEL throughout the school community, such as in hallways through diverse imagery, calming corners, serenity spaces with resources for self-care, and messages of affirmation throughout the school. Ensure that all classroom support staff are also engaging in this work and displaying CRASEL as it relates to their areas. This includes school safety officers, cafeteria staff, cluster teachers, and after-school staff. This will provide a schoolwide cohesive approach. Students should experience CRASEL everywhere they are in the school building and with every adult they encounter.

- **Model, uplift, and maintain collaboration among educators:** Throughout the learning process, the leader should be an active and visible participant. As lead learner, model your learning, exhibit vulnerability, allow model teachers to lead, and join in as a participant. Take staff along with you during supportive walkthroughs, debrief, and plan next steps collaboratively. This is not a task to delegate; to build momentum, dedication, and trust, you have to play an active role as often as you are able.

- **Curate and cultivate distributive leadership across staff, families, and students:** As you engage in this work, take note of staff, families, and students who excel in this work and those who have deep interest. Celebrate their work publicly. Use those staff members in leading professional learning, joining supportive walkthroughs, and modeling videos and lab site classrooms. Identify a CRASEL team to co-lead this work with you. Ensure the team reflects varied constituencies.

- **Track, assess, and monitor school culture qualitatively and quantitatively and regularly seek feedback from the school community:** Through your regular equity audits, you can gather data on progress. Conduct periodic progress monitoring using varied data sets such as attendance, academic data, incidents, suspensions, empathy interviews, and parent and student surveys to identify where progress is happening and where more attention is needed. Share how you are addressing feedback publicly.

- **Exhibit transparency and vulnerability as a leader:** You are the lead learner. Share your own journey with your staff. Before engaging staff in the racial reflection and racial autobiography, share your own. Wherever possible, share your successes and challenges with the CRASEL practices. Model your perseverance through the learning and share when it is difficult for you. This will motivate the school community to engage. Be the change you want to see!

Partnerships

As experiences of students and communities change, you need to widen your net of supports and reach out beyond the expertise of the school building to community-based partners and organizations that can provide the ever changing supports your students and their families need to truly thrive. Addressing research on faith-based and community-based school partnerships, Lynette M. Henry, Julia Bryan, and Carlos P. Zalaquett (2017) write, "school partnerships can be a powerful strategy for alleviating the effects of socioeconomic and educational inequalities, and appear to be effective in helping students in high-poverty schools to succeed academically" (p. 165). With more community school models across the United States, the value and enhancement that a quality community school can provide allows leaders to widen what they are able to offer. In areas of the arts, health services, vision services, dental services, social services, mental health services, family engagement, after-school programs, and more, schools become true hubs of service for the community. Increasingly, school leaders seek out partnerships with these types of organizations to better service families, as well as organizations to support the professional development of staff. University partners can also serve in these roles.

Wherever possible, share your successes and challenges with the CRASEL practices. Model your perseverance through the learning and share when it is difficult for you.

Megan Tschannen-Moran (2014) asserts that trusting, consistent, responsive partnerships that include families, communities, and schools are needed to address "the complex task of educating a diverse group of students in a changing world" (p. 18). Building and sustaining partnerships that function as true trusting relationships do not happen automatically. They take work and effort on all sides—school leader, school, and partners. Community partners should be at the table, analyzing the school's data alongside you and your staff, making decisions, co-creating the school's vision and mission, and planning for their implementation. These relationships are collaborative, communicative, and responsive to changing needs, and they share common goals.

The following are some suggestions for how to maximize partnerships in CRASEL leadership.

- **Select high-quality partnerships and connect partnerships to the mission and schoolwide expectations through collaboration:** When you collaborate with partners to enhance your learning environment and school culture, make sure they are willing to tailor their work to your community's mission, vision, and needs. Be wary of partners who have their own agendas and are unwilling to be flexible in meeting the specific needs of your school community. Wherever possible, include them in the planning so their work seamlessly aligns with the school's mission and vision.

- **Celebrate successes and best practices widely across school and community:** Don't hide the work that you're doing. You are working to shift the mindset of a full school community. This work is only effective if the school community is learning together, collaborating, and co-creating. This is the co-liberation we mentioned earlier. Share successes widely, highlight the voices from the community, share challenges, and, when needed, ask for support. Use school communication platforms, websites, and social media to share the story of what you're doing. Create and share your own narrative!

- **Connect community-based partners with families to meet identified needs:** Ensure your chosen partners are willing to engage with families. If partners have access to community resources or programming for families, communicate this widely and encourage families to take advantage of available resources. Engage community legislators and leaders for collaboration and support. Invite them to events highlighting CRASEL.

- **Provide teachers with input and leadership opportunities in collaboration with partners:** When collaborating with partners, don't work in isolation. Include teachers in the decision-making process when choosing partners and designing programming. The goal is for teachers to embrace partnerships and expectations that will impact them. They are more likely to support the work of partners if they were instrumental in selecting those partners and able to collaborate in their approach, ensuring it meets the needs of their students.

Community partnerships build connection and inclusivity with the surrounding community. When you are a caring advocate who connects with the community, true collaborative partnerships are tangible evidence of that connection.

Conclusion

In this chapter, we deepened our understanding of equity-centered, culturally responsive school leadership, and examined how building and sustaining school culture and maximizing partnerships can help you extend your work schoolwide. We reflected on our work in previous chapters in collaboration with our school communities in self-awareness, self-care, self-management, school and community relationship building, advocacy, and nurturing through high expectations.

Let's consider, in this final chapter, where we are as CRASEL leaders, where our practices are strong, which aspects we've grown in because of the work in previous chapters, and where we want to continue to grow in our practice. The reproducible tool at the end of the chapter, "CRASEL Leadership Reflection" (page 142), can help you reflect on your current practices in becoming a culturally responsive and affirming social-emotional leader and then brainstorm ways you can improve in these practices.

We hope that this book, the work you've engaged in through your learning, and the reflections you've done will serve as a resource you continue to use in your lifelong growth in becoming a culturally responsive and affirming social-emotional leader. After engaging in the following reflective questions, please see the suggested "Potential Action Steps" reproducible (page 143) to help you implement these protocols in your school.

Questions for Reflection and Discussion

Please reflect on the following questions, alone or in a book discussion group, to consider the chapter content and your current and future leadership practices.

1. How has this text helped you develop as a culturally responsive and affirming social-emotional school leader?
2. What specific areas do you want to continue to explore and research? Were there specific scholars, texts, or research mentioned that you want to access and apply?
3. What concerns you in your continued development in this work?
4. What brings you hope?

CRASEL Leadership Reflection

Reflect on your current practices in becoming a culturally responsive and affirming social-emotional leader, and then brainstorm the ways you can improve in these practices.

CRASEL Actions	Glow (area of strength)	Grow (area needing growth)	Aspirations and Committed Next Steps
Self-care, self-awareness, and self-management			
School and community relationship building			
Advocacy			
Nurturing through high expectations			
Culturally responsive sustaining school leadership			
Building and sustaining school culture			
Maximizing partnerships			

Source: Brooks DeCosta, D. (2020). Black principal perspectives on social-emotional learning and culturally responsive leadership in urban schools: The role of beliefs, values, and leadership practices *[Doctoral dissertation, Columbia University]*. Columbia Academic Commons. Accessed at https://academiccommons.columbia.edu/doi/10.7916/d8-qv6y-6846 on July 29, 2024.

The Change You Want to See © 2025 Solution Tree Press • SolutionTree.com
Visit **go.SolutionTree.com/leadership** to download this free reproducible.

Potential Action Steps

In the potential action steps for chapter 8, you have the opportunity to deepen the work and operationalize a practice or practices you and your team would like to begin with. Choose as many or as few as you are able. Consider quality over quantity and think of these possible action steps as opportunities to grow, strengthen, and build on as opposed to steps to take all at once.

- Review the "CRASEL Leadership Reflection" reproducible (page 142) and determine where you might need support. If you are receiving leadership coaching, be sure to include this effort in your growth plan.

- If you are not receiving coaching, consider embarking on this journey with a fellow school leader so you will have someone to debrief with, share practices and challenges with, brainstorm with, and also possibly have intervisitations with between schools.

- Be sure to continue your own learning. Seek out leadership development courses, webinars, conferences, and professional development leadership opportunities in these areas. If any of the scholars cited in this work are presenting, join those sessions.

- Seek out opportunities to visit schools who are already engaging in the work and be sure to learn about their journey and how they managed challenges.

- Stay abreast of new research in CRSL and SEL. Select books and articles that can expand your knowledge. Use the information to share with staff and plan next steps.

- Document your journey. At some point, you may be able to share your best practices with others who want to engage in this work.

- Look for the alignment between CRASEL and your district's leadership evaluation. Determine how you might highlight this work when you are evaluated and be sure to make direct connections to those expectations with your district leadership, as this work is intentional.

Note: Remember, this work will take time. It is continuous and ongoing. Pace yourself according to the needs of your community.

Epilogue

Considering all you have gained through reading this text, what kind of school community are you looking to cultivate and co-create for those you serve? How can you advocate for the most vulnerable in this ever-shifting political climate? And what more can you do to support them and yourself so you may remain resilient, impactful, and able to persevere? We hope that this work has inspired you to consider such questions and gain a better understanding of your role as a leader in your community.

CRASEL is a liberatory approach to leading and learning that holistically meets the needs of the school community. It does so by raising racial and cultural self-awareness and setting high expectations. It attends to students' individual and collective social and emotional needs through agency, social justice, voice, compassion, empathy, and positive relationship building. We've offered the CRASEL framework as an approach to the holistic support you can provide your school communities—while remembering that *you*, school leader, are a part of the school community, and your self-care is as important as the care you provide to others.

We have guided you through our experiences and reflections in relation to the research on SEL and CRSL. We honor the work of the scholars who began this work and imparted the knowledge they've gained, as well as the proven benefits for students. We shared the importance of you serving as the catalyst for this work to occur effectively schoolwide. The same monitoring, system creation, support, observation, feedback, and professional development that a leader would provide to implement any academic program with fidelity are the same requirements for this work. At the same time, there is continual work for you to do within yourself so you can be in service to your community as a model and lead learner in this collective approach.

As we center our social-emotional approach in cultural responsiveness, it is essential for you to do your own internal work to become more self-aware, not only emotionally but also culturally. Similarly, as an emotionally intelligent leader, you are self-aware and recognize and monitor the impact of your emotions on yourself and others, and you must also be culturally self-aware for the same impactful reasons. To nurture through high expectations and as a cornerstone of cultural responsiveness, leaders and educators must believe in the highest potential for all of their students. Deficit lenses negatively impact instructional approaches and efforts to create a safe and nurturing classroom and school environment. We shared this work as collective, an approach that is co-created for the co-liberation of the full school community.

Through trust and strong relationship building, as lead learner, you can cultivate a culture of care that allows everyone to engage in this work with transparency, support, and grace. Your role as advocate for your community will ring true throughout the process. You must believe in the validity of this work, the worthiness of your students and families, and the need for all students, staff, and families to travel this journey together.

We encourage you to continue to use this text and expand your learning by revisiting areas where you may need to grow. This is a lifelong process, and we are all always learning and growing socially, emotionally, and culturally. Be kind to yourself during this process, take care of yourself, take care of one another, and ultimately you will be able to appropriately care for your students and prepare learning environments where all your students can truly thrive. It is our hope that the research, suggestions, and words of experience have been helpful to you and your school communities. And ultimately, we hope for your sustenance, your constant encouragement, your healing, and your restoration as you hold and lift your school communities in a way where everyone—including you—thrives culturally and is affirmed socially and emotionally. The work is monumental, and our future depends on it.

References and Resources

Ahn, M. Y., & Davis, H. H. (2020). Sense of belonging as an indicator of social capital. *International Journal of Sociology and Social Policy, 40*(7/8), 627–642.

Alvarez-Ortiz, L., Haynes, J., & Zacarian, D. (2020, October 1). *Meeting student trauma with an asset-based approach*. ASCD. Accessed at www.ascd.org/el/articles/meeting-student-trauma-with-an-asset-based-approach on August 7, 2024.

Anderson, J. D. (1988). *The education of Blacks in the South, 1860–1935*. Chapel Hill: University of North Carolina Press.

Angelou, M. (1994). *The complete collected poems of Maya Angelou*. New York: Random House.

Arnold, K. A. (2017). Transformational leadership and employee psychological well-being: A review and directions for future research. *Journal of Occupational Health Psychology, 22*(3), 381–393.

Bakosh, L. S., Snow, R. M., Tobias, J. M., Houlihan, J. L., & Barbosa-Leiker, C. (2015). Maximizing mindful learning: Mindful awareness intervention improves elementary school students' quarterly grades. *Mindfulness, 7*, 59–67.

Banwo, B. O., Khalifa, M., & Seashore Louis, K. (2022). Exploring trust: Culturally responsive and positive school leadership. *Journal of Educational Administration, 60*(3), 323–339.

Barnes, T. N., & McCallops, K. (2019). Perceptions of culturally responsive pedagogy in teaching SEL. *Journal for Multicultural Education, 13*(1), 70–81.

Beaumont, K. (2004). *I like myself!* Orlando, FL: Harcourt.

Bell, C. C., & Jenkins, E. J. (1991). Traumatic stress and children. *Journal of Health Care for the Poor and Underserved, 2*(1), 175–185.

Beyoncé, Carter, B. I., Saint Jhn, and Wizkid. (2019). Brown skin girl [Song]. On *The lion king: The gift*. Parkwood; Columbia.

Blanchard, K. (2010). *Building trust: The critical link to a high-involvement, high-energy workplace begins with a common language* [White paper]. Accessed at https://resources.blanchard.com/whitepapers/building-trust-in-the-workplace on November 29, 2023.

Bocala, C., & Boudett, K. P. (2022, February 1). *Looking at data through an equity lens*. ASCD. Accessed at www.ascd.org/el/articles/looking-at-data-through-an-equity-lens on August 7, 2024.

Bohrnstedt, G., Kitmitto, S., Ogut, B., Sherman, D., & Chan, D. (2015). *School composition and the Black-White achievement gap*. Washington, DC: National Center for Education Statistics. Accessed at https://nces.ed.gov/nationsreportcard/subject/studies/pdf/school_composition_and_the_bw_achievement_gap_2015.pdf on March 18, 2024.

Borowski, T. (2019, August). *CASEL's framework for systemic social and emotional learning*. Accessed at https://measuringsel.casel.org/wp-content/uploads/2019/08/AWG-Framework-Series-B.2.pdf on March 18, 2024.

Brackett, M. (2019). *Permission to feel: Unlocking the power of emotions to help our kids, ourselves, and our society thrive*. New York: Celadon Books.

Brackett, M. A., Rivers, S. E., & Salovey, P. (2011). Emotional intelligence: Implications for personal, social, academic, and workplace success. *Social and Personality Psychology Compass*, 5(1), 88–103.

Bray, S., Gunsalus, C. K., Luckman, E. A., Burbules, N. C., & Easter, R. A. (2019, January 9). *Fostering trust in academic departments*. Accessed at www.insidehighered.com/advice/2019/01/10/why-trust-crucial-academe-and-what-you-can-do-cultivate-it-opinion on March 19, 2024.

Brooks DeCosta, D. (2020). *Black principal perspectives on social-emotional learning and culturally responsive leadership in urban schools: The role of beliefs, values, and leadership practices* [Doctoral dissertation, Columbia University]. Columbia Academic Commons. Accessed at https://academiccommons.columbia.edu/doi/10.7916/d8-qv6y-6846 on July 29, 2024.

Brown, C., Maggin, D. M., & Buren, M. (2018). Systematic review of cultural adaptations of school-based social, emotional, and behavioral interventions for students of color. *Education and Treatment of Children*, 41(4), 431–456.

Bryk, A. S., & Schneider, B. (2002). *Trust in schools: A core resource for improvement*. New York: Russell Sage Foundation.

Burroughs, M. D., & Barkauskas, N. J. (2017). Educating the whole child: Social-emotional learning and ethics education. *Ethics and Education*, 12(2), 218–232.

Butler, L. D., Mercer, K. A., McClain-Meeder, K., Horne, D. M., & Dudley, M. (2019). Six domains of self-care: Attending to the whole person. *Journal of Human Behavior in the Social Environment*, 29(1), 107–124.

Calvert, L. (2016). The power of teacher agency: Why we must transform professional learning so that it really supports educator learning. *Journal of Staff Development*, 37(2), 51–56.

Camangian, P., & Cariaga, S. (2022). Social and emotional learning is hegemonic miseducation: Students deserve humanization instead. *Race Ethnicity and Education*, 25(7), 901–921.

Carrero, K. M., Collins, L. W., & Lusk, M. E. (2017). Equity in the evidence base: Demographic sampling in intervention research for students with emotional and behavior disorders. *Behavioral Disorders*, 43(1), 253–261.

Cascade Team. (2023, December 13). *SOAR analysis: What it is & step-by-step guide (2024)*. Accessed at www.cascade.app/blog/soar-analysis-guide on March 20, 2024.

CASEL. (n.d.). *What is the CASEL framework?* Accessed at https://casel.org/fundamentals-of-sel/what-is-the-casel-framework/ on March 18, 2024.

Cavanagh, T., Macfarlane, A., Glynn, T., & Macfarlane, S. (2012). Creating peaceful and effective schools through a culture of care. *Discourse: Studies in the Cultural Politics of Education*, 33(3), 443–455.

Comer, J. P., & Gates, H. L., Jr. (2004). *Leave no child behind: Preparing today's youth for tomorrow's world*. New Haven, CT: Yale University Press.

Communities for Just Schools Fund. (2020, May 7). *When SEL is used as another form of policing*. Accessed at https://medium.com/@justschools/when-sel-is-used-as-another-form-of-policing-fa53cf85dce4 on July 31, 2024.

Community Tool Box. (n.d.). Section 14. *SWOT analysis: Strengths, weaknesses, opportunities, and threats*. Accessed at https://ctb.ku.edu/en/table-of-contents/assessment/assessing-community-needs-and-resources/swot-analysis/main on March 20, 2024.

Cooper, C. W. (2009). Performing cultural work in demographically changing schools: Implications for expanding transformative leadership frameworks. *Educational Administration Quarterly*, 45(5), 694–724.

Creating a Respectful and Open World for Natural Hair Act of 2022, H.R.2116, 117th Congress. (2022). Accessed at www.congress.gov/bill/117th-congress/house-bill/2116/text on August 16, 2024.

Cross, D., Vance, L. A., Kim, Y. J., Ruchard, A. L., Fox, N., Jovanovic, T., et al. (2018). Trauma exposure, PTSD, and parenting in a community sample of low-income, predominantly African American mothers and children. *Psychological Trauma: Theory, Research, Practice and Policy*, 10(3), 327–335.

Cutts, Q. M. (2020). More than casual concern: Critical Black pedagogical excellence and the Asa G. Hilliard, III teacher preparation framework. *International Journal of Qualitative Studies in Education*, 33(7), 709–728.

Delpit, L. (2006). *Other people's children: Cultural conflict in the classroom*. New York: New Press.

DeMatthews, D., Carrola, P., Reyes, P., & Knight, D. (2021). School leadership burnout and job-related stress: Recommendations for district administrators and principals. *The Clearing House: A Journal of Educational Strategies, Issues and Ideas, 94*(4), 159–167. https://doi.org/10.1080/00098655.2021.1894083

DeMatthews, D., & Mawhinney, H. (2014). Social justice leadership and inclusion: Exploring challenges in an urban district struggling to address inequities. *Educational Administration Quarterly, 50*(5), 844–881.

Drago-Severson, E. (2004). *Helping teachers learn: Principal leadership for adult growth and development*. Thousand Oaks, CA: Corwin.

Drago-Severson, E. (2008). *4 practices serve as pillars for adult learning: Learning-oriented leadership offers a promising way to support growth*. Oxford, OH: National Staff Development Council. Accessed at https://cahnfellowsprograms.org/wp-content/uploads/2021/03/1A-drago-severson-JSD-2008.pdf on March 20, 2024.

Drago-Severson, E. (2009). *Leading adult learning: Supporting adult development in our schools*. Thousand Oaks, CA: Corwin.

Dückers, M. L. A., Yzermans, C. J., Jong, W., & Boin, A. (2017). Psychosocial crisis management: The unexplored intersection of crisis leadership and psychosocial support. *Risk Hazards and Crisis Public Policy, 8*(2), 94–112.

Dunbar, P. L. (1922). *The complete poems of Paul Laurence Dunbar*. New York: Dodd, Mead.

Durlak, J. A., Domitrovich, C. E., Weissberg, R. P., & Gullotta, T. P. (Eds.). (2015). *Handbook of social and emotional learning: Research and practice*. New York: Guilford Press.

Esimai, C. (2018, February 15). *Great leadership starts with self-awareness*. Forbes. Accessed at www.forbes.com/sites/ellevate/2018/02/15/self-awareness-being-more-of-what-makes-you-great/?sh=1d94f80540dd on March 19, 2024.

Espelage, D. L., King, M. T., & Colbert, C. L. (2018). Emotional intelligence and school-based bullying prevention and intervention. In K. V. Keefer, J. D. A. Parker, & D. H. Saklofske (Eds.), *Emotional intelligence in education: Integrating research with practice* (pp. 217–242). Cham, Switzerland: Springer International.

Evertson, C. M., & Weinstein, C. S. (Eds.). (2006). *Handbook of classroom management: Research, practice, and contemporary issues*. Mahwah, NJ: Erlbaum.

Folsom, J., Espolt, A., Moyle, P., Leonard, K., Busselle, R., Pate, C., et al. (2021, April). *Reimagining excellence: A blueprint for integrating social and emotional well-being and academic excellence in schools*. San Francisco: Region 13 Comprehensive Center. Accessed at https://files.eric.ed.gov/fulltext/ED613077.pdf on March 19, 2024.

Franklin, A. J., Boyd-Franklin, N., & Kelly, S. (2006). Racism and invisibility: Race-related stress, emotional abuse and psychological trauma for people of color. *Journal of Emotional Abuse, 6*(2–3), 9–30.

Freire, P. (1973). *Education for critical consciousness*. New York: Seabury Press.

Freire, P. (2018). *Pedagogy of the oppressed* (50th anniversary ed.; M. Bergman Ramos, Trans.). New York: Bloomsbury Academic. (Original work published 1968)

Furman, G. (2012). Social justice leadership as praxis: Developing capacities through preparation programs. *Educational Administration Quarterly, 48*(2), 191–229.

García-Sancho, E., Dhont, K., Salguero, J. M., & Fernández-Berrocal, P. (2017). The personality basis of aggression: The mediating role of anger and the moderating role of emotional intelligence. *Scandinavian Journal of Psychology, 58*(4), 333–340.

Garner, P. W., Mahatmya, D., Brown, E. L., & Vesely, C. K. (2014). Promoting desirable outcomes among culturally and ethnically diverse children in social-emotional learning programs: A multilevel heuristic model. *Educational Psychology Review, 26*(1), 165–189.

Gay, G. (1994). Coming of age ethnically: Teaching young adolescents of color. *Theory Into Practice, 33*(3), 149–155.

Gay, G. (2002). Preparing for culturally responsive teaching. *Journal of Teacher Education, 53*(2), 106–116.

Gay, G. (2010). *Culturally responsive teaching: Theory, research, and practice* (2nd ed.). New York: Teachers College Press.

Gay, G., & Kirkland, K. (2003). Developing cultural critical consciousness and self-reflection in preservice teacher education. *Theory Into Practice, 42*(3), 181–187.

Godfrey, E. B., Santos, C. E., & Burson, E. (2019). For better or worse? System-justifying beliefs in sixth-grade predict trajectories of self-esteem and behavior across early adolescence. *Child Development, 90*(1), 180–195.

Goff, P. A., Jackson, M. C., Di Leone, B. A. L., Culotta, C. M., & DiTomasso, N. A. (2014). The essence of innocence: Consequences of dehumanizing Black children. *Journal of Personality and Social Psychology, 106*(4), 526–545.

Goldring, R., Taie, S., & O'Rear, I. (2018). *Principal attrition and mobility: Results from the 2016–17 principal follow-up survey. First look* (NCES 2018-066). National Center for Education Statistics. Accessed at https://files.eric.ed.gov/fulltext/ED585933.pdf on August 5, 2024.

Goleman, D. (1995). *Emotional intelligence*. New York: Bantam Books.

Goleman, D. (2006). *Social intelligence: The new science of human relationships*. New York: Bantam Books.

Gómez-Leal, R., Holzer, A. A., Bradley, C., Fernández-Berrocal, P., & Patti, J. (2022). The relationship between emotional intelligence and leadership in school leaders: A systematic review. *Cambridge Journal of Education, 52*(1), 1–21.

Gooden, M. A. (2005). The role of an African American principal in an urban information technology high school. *Educational Administration Quarterly, 41*(4), 630–650.

Gooden, M. A. (2021). Why every principal should write a racial autobiography. *Educational Leadership, 78*(7), 32–37.

Gooden, M. A., & Dantley, M. (2012). Centering race in a framework for leadership preparation. *Journal of Research on Leadership Education, 7*(2), 237–253. https://doi.org/10.1177/1942775112455266

Gooden, M. A., Khalifa, M., Arnold, N. W., Brown, K. D., Meyers, C. V., & Welsh, R. O. (2023). *A culturally responsive school leadership approach to developing equity-centered principals: Considerations for principal pipelines*. Wallace Foundation. Accessed at https://wallacefoundation.org/sites/default/files/2023-07/Culturally-responsive-school-leadership-approach_06.29.FINALforposting.pdf on August 9, 2024.

Gooden, M. A., & O'Doherty, A. (2015). Do you see what I see? Fostering aspiring leaders' racial awareness. *Urban Education, 50*(2), 225–255.

Greenberg, M. T., Domitrovich, C. E., Weissberg, R. P., & Durlak, J. A. (2017). Social and emotional learning as a public health approach to education. *The Future of Children, 27*(1), 13–32.

Hammond, Z. (2015). *Culturally responsive teaching and the brain: Promoting authentic engagement and rigor among culturally and linguistically diverse students*. Thousand Oaks, CA: Corwin.

Harding, J. F., & Sibley, C. G. (2013). The palliative function of system justification: Concurrent benefits versus longer-term costs to wellbeing. *Social Indicators Research, 113*(1), 401–418.

Harrison, L., Hurd, E., & Brinegar, K. (2021). But is it really about critical race theory? The attack on teaching about systemic racism and why we must care. *Middle School Journal, 52*(4), 2–3.

Henry, L. M., Bryan, J., & Zalaquett, C. P. (2017). The effects of a counselor-led, faith-based, school-family-community partnership on student achievement in a high-poverty urban elementary school. *Journal of Multicultural Counseling and Development, 45*(3), 162–182.

Higgins, K. M., & Moule, J. (2009). "No more Mr. Nice Guy": Preservice teachers' conflict with classroom management in a predominantly African-American urban elementary school. *Multicultural Perspectives, 11*(3), 132–138.

High Tech High Graduate School of Education. (n.d.). *Empathy interviews*. Accessed at https://hthgse.edu/resources/empathy-interviews/#flipbook-empathy-interviews/2/ on August 7, 2024.

Hitt, D. H., Woodruff, D., Meyers, C. V., & Zhu, G. (2018). Principal competencies that make a difference: Identifying a model for leaders of school turnaround. *Journal of School Leadership, 28*(1), 56–81. https://doi.org/10.1177/105268461802800103

Hoffmann, J. D., Ivcevic, Z., & Brackett, M. A. (2018). Building emotionally intelligent schools: From preschool to high school and beyond. In K. V. Keefer, J. D. A. Parker, & D. H. Saklofske (Eds.), *Emotional intelligence in education: Integrating research with practice* (pp. 173–198). Cham, Switzerland: Springer International.

Hollins, C. D., & Govan, I. M. (2015). *Diversity, equity, and inclusion: Strategies for facilitating conversations on race*. Lanham, MD: Rowman and Littlefield.

Horsford, S. D. (2009). From Negro student to Black superintendent: Counternarratives on segregation and desegregation. *Journal of Negro Education, 78*(2), 172–187.

Horsford, S. D., Grosland, T., & Gunn, K. M. (2011). Pedagogy of the personal and professional: Toward a framework for culturally relevant leadership. *Journal of School Leadership, 21*(4), 582–606.

Howard, T. C. (2019). *Why race and culture matter in schools: Closing the achievement gap in America's classrooms* (2nd ed.). New York: Teachers College Press.

Hughes, L. (1994). *The collected poems of Langston Hughes* (A. Rampersad, Ed.). New York: Vintage.

Hughes, M., Kiecolt, K. J., Keith, V. M., & Demo, D. H. (2015). Racial identity and well-being among African Americans. *Social Psychology Quarterly, 78*(1), 25–48.

Hutcherson, C. A., Seppala, E. M., & Gross, J. J. (2008). Loving-kindness meditation increases social connectedness. *Emotion, 8*(5), 720–724. https://doi.org/10.1037/a0013237

Ieva, K., & Beasley, J. (2022). Dismantling racism through collaborative consultation: Promoting culturally affirming educator SEL. *Theory Into Practice, 61*(2), 236–249.

Irwin, V., De La Rosa, J., Wang, K., Hein, S., Zhang, J., Burr, R., et al. (2022). *Report on the condition of education 2022*. Washington, DC: National Center for Education Statistics. Accessed at https://nces.ed.gov/pubs2022/2022144.pdf on March 19, 2024.

Juvonen, J., & Knifsend, C. (2016). School-based peer relationships and achievement motivation. In K. R. Wentzel & D. B. Miele (Eds.), *Handbook of motivation at school* (2nd ed., pp. 231–250). New York: Routledge.

Khalifa, M. (2012). A "re"-new-"ed" paradigm in successful urban school leadership: Principal as community leader. *Educational Administration Quarterly, 48*(3), 424–467.

Khalifa, M. A., Gooden, M. A., & Davis, J. E. (2016). Culturally responsive school leadership: A synthesis of the literature. *Review of Educational Research, 86*(4), 1272–1311. http://dx.doi.org/doi:10.3102/0034654316630383

Knight-Manuel, M. G., & Marciano, J. E. (2019). *Classroom cultures: Equitable schooling for racially diverse youth*. New York: Teachers College Press.

Kwon, K., Hanrahan, A. R., & Kupzyk, K. A. (2017). Emotional expressivity and emotion regulation: Relation to academic functioning among elementary school children. *School Psychology Quarterly, 32*(1), 75–88.

Ladson-Billings, G. (1995a). But that's just good teaching! The case for culturally relevant pedagogy. *Theory Into Practice, 34*(3), 159–165.

Ladson-Billings, G. (1995b). Toward a theory of culturally relevant pedagogy. *American Educational Research Journal, 32*(3), 465–491. http://dx.doi.org/https://doi.org/10.3102%2F00028312032003465

Lalor, A. D. (2020, October 22). *3 steps to developing an asset-based approach to teaching*. Edutopia. Accessed at www.edutopia.org/article/3-steps-developing-asset-based-approach-teaching on August 7, 2024.

LaPoint, V., Ellison, C. M., & Boykin, A. W. (2006). Educating the whole child: The talent quest model for educational policy and practice. *The Journal of Negro Education, 75*(3), 373–388.

Larson, K. E., Pas, E. T., Bradshaw, C. P., Rosenberg, M. S., & Day-Vines, N. L. (2018). Examining how proactive management and culturally responsive teaching relate to student behavior: Implications for measurement and practice. *School Psychology Review, 47*(2), 153–166.

Lee, A. T., & Haskins, N. H. (2022). Toward a culturally humble practice: Critical consciousness as an antecedent. *Journal of Counseling and Development, 100*(1), 104–112.

Leithwood, K. A. (2014). The principal's role in teacher development. In M. Fulland & A. Hargreaves (Eds.), *Teacher development and educational change* (pp. 86–103). New York: Routledge.

Leung-Gagné, M., McCombs, J., Scott, C., & Losen, D. J. (2022, September 30). *Pushed out: Trends and disparities in out-of-school suspension*. Learning Policy Institute. https://doi.org/10.54300/235.277

Little, S., & Maunder, R. E. (2021). Why we should train teachers on the impact of childhood trauma on classroom behaviour. *Educational and Child Psychology, 38*(1), 54–61. https://doi.org/10.53841/bpsecp.2021.38.1.54

Lomotey, K. (1989). Cultural diversity in the school: Implications for principals. *NASSP Bulletin, 73*(521), 81–88.

Lomotey, K. (1993). African-American principals: Bureaucrat/administrators and ethno-humanists. *Urban Education, 27*(4), 394–412.

Lomotey, K. (2019). Research on the leadership of Black women principals: Implications for Black students. *Educational Researcher, 48*(6), 336–348.

Lomotey, K., & Lowery, K. (2014). Black students, urban schools, and Black principals: Leadership practices that reduce disenfranchisement. In H. R. Milner IV & K. Lomotey (Eds.), *Handbook of urban education* (pp. 325–350). New York: Routledge.

Lomotey, K., & Weiler, J. (2021). Promoting and limiting voice: The influence of web-based platforms on public policy discourse. *Urban Education, 56*(4), 547–551.

MacDonald, E. (2011). When nice won't suffice: Honest discourse is key to shifting school culture. *Journal of Staff Development, 32*(3), 45–47, 51.

Madda, M. J. (2019, May 15). *Dena Simmons: Without context, social-emotional learning can backfire*. Accessed at www.edsurge.com/news/2019-05-15-dena-simmons-without-context-social-emotional-learning-can-backfire on March 19, 2024.

Mansfield, K. C., Welton, A., & Halx, M. (2018). Listening to student voice: Toward a more holistic approach to school leadership. *Journal of Ethical Educational Leadership, 5*(2), 1–18.

Marshall, S. L., & Khalifa, M. A. (2018). Humanizing school communities: Culturally responsive leadership in the shaping of curriculum and instruction. *Journal of Educational Administration, 56*(5), 533–545. https://doi.org/10.1108/JEA-01-2018-0018

McFarland, J., Hussar, B., Zhang, J., Wang, X., Wang, K., Hein, S., et al. (2019). *The condition of education 2019*. Washington, DC: National Center for Education Statistics. Accessed at https://nces.ed.gov/pubs2019/2019144.pdf on March 19, 2024.

Mid-Atlantic Equity Consortium. (2021). *Equity audit*. Accessed at https://maec.org/equity-audit on August 7, 2024.

Milner, H. R. (2006). Preservice teachers' learning about cultural and racial diversity: Implications for urban education. *Urban Education*, *41*(4), 343–375.

Mitchell, V. (1992). African-American students in exemplary urban high schools: The interaction of school practices and student actions. In M. Saravia-Shore & S. F. Arvizu (Eds.), *Cross-cultural literacy: Ethnographies of communication in multiethnic classrooms* (pp. 19–36). New York: Routledge.

Molano, A., Harker, A., & Cristancho, J. C. (2018). Effects of indirect exposure to homicide events on children's mental health: Evidence from urban settings in Colombia. *Journal of Youth and Adolescence*, *47*(10), 2060–2072.

Moorosi, P., Fuller, K., & Reilly, E. C. (2018). Leadership and intersectionality: Constructions of successful leadership among Black women school principals in three different contexts. *Management in Education*, *32*(4), 152–159.

Moreno, A. J., Nagasawa, M. K., & Schwartz, T. (2019). Social and emotional learning and early childhood education: Redundant terms? *Contemporary Issues in Early Childhood*, *20*(3), 221–235. https://doi.org/10.1177/1463949118768040

Morgan, T. L., & Cieminski, A. B. (2023). Critical reflection to develop transformative consciousness of racial differences. *Professional Development in Education*, *49*(4), 634–650.

Morris, J. E. (1999). What is the future of predominantly Black urban schools? The politics of race in urban education policy. *Phi Delta Kappan*, *81*(4), 316–319.

Morris, J. E., & Monroe, C. R. (2009). Why study the U.S. South? The nexus of race and place in investigating Black student achievement. *Educational Researcher*, *38*(1), 21–36.

Muhammad, G. (2018). A plea for identity and criticality: Reframing literacy learning standards through a four-layered equity model. *Journal of Adolescent and Adult Literacy*, *62*(2), 137–142.

Muhammad, G. (2020). *Cultivating genius: An equity framework for culturally and historically responsive literacy*. New York: Scholastic.

Muhammad, G. (2023). *Unearthing joy: A guide to culturally and historically responsive teaching and learning*. New York: Scholastic.

Mutch, C. (2015). The impact of the Canterbury earthquakes on schools and school leaders: Educational leaders become crisis managers. *Journal of Educational Leadership, Policy and Practice*, *30*(2), 39–55.

National Association of Elementary School Principals. (2021, March 6). *New school equity audit tool*. Accessed at www.naesp.org/news/new-school-equity-audit-tool/ on August 7, 2024.

National Institute of Mental Health. (n.d.). *Caring for your mental health*. Accessed at https://www.nimh.nih.gov/health/topics/caring-for-your-mental-health on August 9, 2024.

Nelsestuen, K., & Smith, J. (2020). Empathy interviews. *The Learning Professional*, *41*(5), 59–62.

New York State Education Department. (2019). *Culturally responsive-sustaining education framework*. Accessed at www.nysed.gov/crs/framework on August 9, 2024.

Nöthling, J., Suliman, S., Martin, L., Simmons, C., & Seedat, S. (2019). Differences in abuse, neglect, and exposure to community violence in adolescents with and without PTSD and depression. *Journal of Interpersonal Violence*, *34*(21–22), 4357–4383. https://doi.org/10.1177/0886260516674944

Oliveira, S., Roberto, M. S., Pereira, N. S., Marques-Pinto, A., & Veiga-Simão, A. M. (2021). Impacts of social and emotional learning interventions for teachers on teachers' outcomes: A systematic review with meta-analysis. *Frontiers in Psychology*, *12*. https://doi.org/10.3389/fpsyg.2021.677217

O'Neil, J. (1997). Building schools as communities: A conversation with James Comer. *Educational Leadership*, *54*(8), 6–10.

Payton, J. W., Wardlaw, D. M., Graczyk, P. A., Bloodworth, M. R., Tompsett, C. J., & Weissberg, R. P. (2000). Social and emotional learning: A framework for promoting mental health and reducing risk behavior in children and youth. *The Journal of School Health*, *70*(5), 179–185.

People and Organizational Development. (n.d.). *Self-awareness*. Accessed at https://pod.admin.ox.ac.uk/self-awareness on August 9, 2024.

Peters, A. L. (2019). Desegregation and the (dis)integration of Black school leaders: Reflections on the impact of *Brown v. Board of Education* on Black education. *Peabody Journal of Education*, *94*(5), 521–534.

Powell, R., Cantrell, S. C., Correll, P. K., & Malo-Juvera, V. (2017). *Culturally responsive instruction observation protocol* (4th ed.). Lexington: University of Kentucky. Accessed at www.iasp.org/wp-content/uploads/2022/02/criop_final_2018-3.pdf on March 20, 2024.

Radd, S. I., Generett, G. G., Gooden, M. A., & Theoharis, G. (2021). *Five practices for equity-focused school leadership*. Alexandria, VA: ASCD.

Ray, J., Pijanowski, J., & Lasater, K. (2020). The self-care practices of school principals. *Journal of Educational Administration*, *58*(4), 435–451.

Rhythm. (n.d.). In *Merriam-Webster's online dictionary*. Accessed at www.merriam-webster.com/dictionary/rhythm on March 21, 2024.

Rivera-McCutchen, R. L. (2021). *Radical care: Leading for justice in urban schools*. New York: Teachers College Press.

Salovey, P., & Mayer, J. D. (1990a). *Emotional intelligence*. New York: Baywood.

Salovey, P., & Mayer, J. D. (1990b). Emotional intelligence. *Imagination, Cognition and Personality*, *9*(3), 185–211. https://doi.org/10.2190/DUGG-P24E-52WK-6CDG

Salovey, P., Stroud, L. R., Woolery, A., & Epel, E. S. (2002). Perceived emotional intelligence, stress reactivity, and symptom reports: Further explorations using the Trait Meta-Mood Scale. *Psychology and Health*, *17*(5), 611–627.

Scholastic Art. (2021, December). *Materials with meaning featuring Bisa Butler*. Accessed at https://art.scholastic.com/issues/2021-22/120121.html on August 7, 2024.

Scott, J., Moses, M. S., Finnigan, K. S., Trujillo, T., & Jackson, D. D. (2017). *Law and order in school and society: How discipline and policing policies harm students of color, and what we can do about it*. Boulder, CO: National Education Policy Center. Accessed at https://nepc.colorado.edu/libraries/pdf.js/web/viewer.html?file=https://nepc.colorado.edu/sites/default/files/publications/PB%20Law%20and%20Order_0.pdf on March 19, 2024.

Simmons, D. (2019a, October 1). *How to be an antiracist educator*. Accessed at www.ascd.org/publications/newsletters/education-update/oct19/vol61/num10/How-to-Be-an-Antiracist-Educator.aspx on March 20, 2024.

Simmons, D. (2019b, April 1). *Why we can't afford whitewashed social-emotional learning*. Accessed at www.ascd.org/el/articles/why-we-cant-afford-whitewashed-social-emotional-learning on March 20, 2024.

Simmons, D. N. (2019c). You can't be emotionally intelligent without being culturally responsive: Why FCS must employ both to meet the needs of our nation. *Journal of Family and Consumer Sciences*, *111*(2), 7–16. https://doi.org/10.14307/JFCS111.2.7

Simmons, D. N., Brackett, M. A., & Adler, N. (2018, June). *Applying an equity lens to social, emotional, and academic development*. University Park, PA: Edna Bennett Pierce Prevention Research Center. Accessed at https://prevention.psu.edu/wp-content/uploads/2022/05/rwjf446338-EquityLens.pdf on March 20, 2024.

Singleton, G. E., & Hays, C. (2008). Beginning courageous conversations about race. In M. Pollock (Ed.), *Everyday antiracism: Getting real about race in school* (pp. 18–23). New York: The New Press.

Thapa, A., Cohen, J., Guffey, S., & Higgins-D'Alessandro, A. (2013). A review of school climate research. *Review of Educational Research*, *83*(3), 357–385.

Tillman, L. C. (2004). African American principals and the legacy of *Brown*. *Review of Research in Education*, *28*, 101–146.

Tillman, L. C. (2008). The scholarship of Dr. Asa G. Hilliard, III: Implications for Black principal leadership. *Review of Educational Research*, *78*(3), 589–607.

Tschannen-Moran, M. (2014). *Trust matters: Leadership for successful schools*. San Francisco: Jossey-Bass.

Urick, A., Carpenter, B. W., & Eckert, J. (2021). Confronting COVID: Crisis leadership, turbulence, and self-care. *Frontiers in Education*, *6*. https://doi.org/10.3389/feduc.2021.642861

U.S. Department of Education Office for Civil Rights. (2014, March 21). *Civil rights data collection: Data snapshot—School discipline*. Washington, DC: Author. Accessed at https://civilrightsdata.ed.gov/assets/downloads/2011-12_CRDC-School-Discipline-Snapshot.pdf on March 20, 2024.

Walker, V. S. (2009). Second-class integration: A historical perspective for a contemporary agenda. *Harvard Educational Review*, *79*(2), 269–284.

Walker, V. S., & Snarey, J. R. (Eds.). (2004). *Race-ing moral formation: African American perspectives on care and justice*. New York: Teachers College Press.

Wang, D., & Hagins, M. (2016). Perceived benefits of yoga among urban school students: A qualitative analysis. *Evidence-Based Complementary and Alternative Medicine*. https://doi.org/10.1155/2016/8725654

Ward Randolph, A., & Robinson, D. V. (2019). De facto desegregation in the urban North: Voices of African American teachers and principals on employment, students, and community in Columbus, Ohio, 1940 to 1980. *Urban Education*, *54*(10), 1403–1430.

Warren, E. & Supreme Court Of The United States. (1954) U.S. Reports: Brown v. Board of Education, 347 U.S. 483. [Periodical] Accessed at www.loc.gov/item/usrep347483/.

Weaver, T., Jr. (2020, June 16). *Antiracism in social-emotional learning: Why it's not enough to talk the talk*. Accessed at www.edsurge.com/news/2020-06-16-antiracism-in-social-emotional-learning-why-it-s-not-enough-to-talk-the-talk on March 20, 2024.

Weiler, J. R., & Lomotey, K. (2022). Defining rigor in justice-oriented EdD programs: Preparing leaders to disrupt and transform schools. *Educational Administration Quarterly, 58*(1), 110–140.

Williams-Wyche, S., Fergus, M., & Djurovich, A. (2016). *Educating for the future 2016: Update and policy guide*. St. Paul: Minnesota Office of Higher Education.

Willis, J. (2016, December 7). *Using brain breaks to restore students' focus*. Edutopia. Accessed at www.edutopia.org/article/brain-breaks-restore-student-focus-judy-willis/ on March 20, 2024.

Winton, S. (2013). From zero tolerance to student success in Ontario, Canada. *Educational Policy, 27*(3), 467–498. http://dx.doi.org/10.1177/0895904812453994

Yale Center for Emotional Intelligence. (n.d.). *RULER*. Accessed at https://medicine.yale.edu/childstudy/services/community-and-schools-programs/center-for-emotional-intelligence/training/ruler/ on August 22, 2024.

Yan, R. (2020). The influence of working conditions on principal turnover in K–12 public schools. *Educational Administration Quarterly, 56*(1), 89–122.

Young, J. L., Young, J. R., & Butler, B. R. (2018). A student saved is NOT a dollar earned: A meta-analysis of school disparities in discipline practice toward Black children. *Taboo, 17*(4), 95–112. https://doi.org/10.31390/taboo.17.4.06

Zacarian, D., Alvarez-Ortiz, L., & Haynes, J. (2018, May 24). *5 elements of a positive classroom environment for students living with adversity*. ASCD. Accessed at www.ascd.org/blogs/five-elements-of-a-positive-classroom-environment-for-students-living-with-adversity on August 7, 2024.

Zembylas, M., & Matias, C. E. (2023). White racial ignorance and refusing culpability: How the emotionalities of Whiteness ignore race in teacher education. *Race, Ethnicity and Education, 26*(4), 456–477.

Zins, J. E., & Elias, M. J. (2007). Social and emotional learning: Promoting the development of all students. *Journal of Educational and Psychological Consultation, 17*(2–3), 233–255.

Index

A

academic achievement
    advocacy and, 107–108
    CRSL/SEL and, 21–22, 26
    culture of care and, 38
    expectations for, 119
    impact of relationships on, 11–12
    racial reflection and, 73–74
    relationships and, 84, 91, 93
accountability, 20–21
    collaboration and, 85–86
    community, 83
    mindfulness practice and, 54
    performance measures and, 21
    social capital and, 108–109
    stress related to, 57
activism, 2.
    See also advocacy
Adler, N., 40
advocacy, 2, 101–113
    committing to, 45, 46
    for communities, 90
    potential action steps for, 113
    questions for reflection on, 111
    racial reflection and, 75
    social justice leadership and, 104–105
    Words From a Principal on, 102–103, 109–110
    Words From a Professor on, 103–104
"Advocacy Leadership Reflection"
    reproducible, 109, 112
affirmation stations, 41
agency
    emotional intelligence and, 12
    social capital and, 108–109
    student and family, 95–96
    teacher, 94–95
Ahn, M. Y., 108
allies, 84
Alvarez-Ortiz, L., 107
"Antiracism in Social-Emotional Learning: Why It's Not Enough to Talk the Talk" (Weaver), 17
Arnold, N. W., 55
asset-based approaches, 106–107

B

Banwo, B. O., 87
Beasley, J., 94
Beaumont, K., 41
behavior
    discipline gap and, 38–39
    emotion regulation and, 13
    modeling, 57–59
    self-awareness, self-management, and, 57–59
belonging, 13
    behavior and, 38
    race/ethnicity and, 71–72
    relational trust and, 87
biases.
    See also racism
    discipline practices and, 117, 120, 122
    implicit, 40, 43
    leadership and, 71–72
    teaching about, prohibitions of, 37
Blanchard, K., 91
Blueprint, 24, 62
Bocala, C., 107
Boudett, K. P., 107

Boyd-Franklin, N., 18
Boykin, A. W., 35–36
Brackett, M. A., 12, 24–25, 40, 58
Brinegar, K., 37
Brooks DeCosta study, 31–32
    on caring for community, 43–44
    on caring for self, 44–45
    on caring for students, 43
    CRASEL framework, 45–48
    themes of leaders' perspectives in, 41–45
Brown, C., 38
Brown, E. L., 39
Brown, K. D., 55
Brown v. Board of Education, 119, 126
Bryan, J., 139
Bryk, A. S., 86
Building a Community of Trust Through Racial Awareness, 72
"Building Staff Trust in a High Accountability Environment," 91–93
"Building Trust: The Critical Link to a High-Involvement, High-Energy Workplace Begins With a Common Language" (Blanchard), 91
Buren, M., 38
burnout, 40, 59
Butler, B. R., 17, 41
Butler, L. D., 59–60
Butts, C. O., III, 4
buy-in, 20

C

Cahn Fellowship, 83–84
Calvert, L., 94–95
Cantrell, S. C., 110
Carrola, P., 60, 61
Caruso, D., 33–34
Casade Team, 110
CASEL framework, 12–13, 31–32.
    See also Collaborative for Academic, Social, and Emotional Learning (CASEL)
Cavanagh, T., 19–20
Charter, 24, 120, 121–122
classroom management, 37–39
co-creation, 93–96
    school culture and, 137
co-liberation, 93–96
    advocacy and, 104–105
    high expectations and, 118–119
collaboration
    with partners, 140
    providing time for, 94
    relationship building and, 84–85
    school culture and, 138
    vision and, 56
Collaborative for Academic, Social, and Emotional Learning (CASEL), 11
    CASEL framework and, 12–13
Comer, J., 11–12
Comer Process, 11–12
commitment, 20
communication
    with communities, 88
    connecting school and, 88, 89–90
    empathy interviews, 109–110
    structures/systems for, 88, 90–91
communities
    advocacy and, 101–113
    belonging and, 71–72
    caring for, 42, 43–44
    in creating safe environments, 120–121
    leaders' self-awareness and, 58–59
    partnerships with, 139–140
    relationship building and, 83–99
    relationship strengthening with, 87–91
    social activism for, 105–106
    transformational leadership and, 21
"Community Relationship-Building Reflection," 91, 98
Community Tool Box, 110
compassion
    relational trust and, 87
    transformational leadership and, 21–22
competence, 86
connection, 13, 39
    belonging and, 13, 38, 71–72, 87
    direct, 88, 90–91
    looking for opportunities for, 89
    relational trust and, 87
context, 16
    invisibility syndrome and, 18–19
conversations, courageous, 76
    empathy interviews and, 107–108
Correll, P. K., 110
COVID-19 pandemic, 13
    advocacy in, 102–103
    crisis leadership and, 59
CRASEL.
    See culturally responsive and affirming social-emotional leadership (CRASEL)
CRASEL framework, 45–48
    advocacy, 101–113
    building school and community relationships, 83–99
    cultural responsiveness, 115–131
    nurturing through high expectations, 115–131
    partnerships, 133–143
    racial reflection, 67–81
    school culture, 133–143
    self-care, 53–65
"CRASEL Leadership Reflection" reproducible, 141, 142
crisis leadership, 59
critical consciousness, 34, 74–75, 95
CROWN Act (Texas), 117–118
CRSE.
    See culturally responsive sustaining education (CRSE)
CRSL.
    See culturally responsive school leadership (CRSL)
CRSL framework, 31
Cultivating Genius (Muhammad), 41, 124, 127
cultural, 2
culturally relevant pedagogy, 19, 35
culturally responsive and affirming social-emotional leadership (CRASEL), 145–146.
    See also CRASEL framework
    approaches to discipline in, 37–39
    bridging CRSL and SEL with, 31–51
    Brooks DeCosta study on, 31–32
    caring for community in, 41, 43–44
    caring for self in, 41, 44–45
    caring for students in, 41, 43
    culture of care and, 36–41
    key terms in, 34–36
    origins of, 41–45
    potential action steps for, 50–51
    practicing, 31–51
    reflection and discussion questions on, 49
    Words From a Principal on, 32–33
    Words From a Professor on, 33–34
Culturally Responsive Instruction Observation Protocol (Powell, Cantrell, Correll, and Malo-Juvera), 110
culturally responsive pedagogy, 19, 35
culturally responsive school leadership (CRSL), 1–2, 145–146

bridging with CRASEL, 31–51
definition of, 19–20, 35
key terms in, 34–36
routines and practices in implementing, 22–26
self-care and, 55–56
transformational leaders and, 20–22
culturally responsive sustaining education (CRSE), 35
CRASEL framework on, 45, 47
Culturally Responsive Teaching and the Brain (Hammond), 76
cultural responsiveness, 115–131
before *Brown v. Board*, 119
high expectations and, 118–119
potential action steps on, 131
practices for, 125–129
questions for reflection on, 129
safe and nurturing environments and, 120–125
self-awareness and, 74–75
Words From a Principal on, 116–117, 128–129
Words From a Professor on, 117–118
culture
building and sustaining school, 45, 47, 133–143
building common understandings of, 75
nurturing, high expectations and, 115–131
potential action steps for, 143
questions for reflection on, 141
Words From a Principal on, 133–134
Words From a Professor on, 135–136
culture of care, 36–41
approaches to culture and, 40–41
caring for community and, 42, 43–44
caring for students and, 42, 43
culturally responsive leadership and, 19–20
self-care and, 42, 44–45
transformational leadership and, 20–22

D

data analysis, 95
determining student needs and, 126–127
equity audits and, 110
students' instructions needs and, 120, 123
Davenport, S. L., 78
Davis, H. H., 108
Davis, J. E., 19, 31, 38, 72–73, 104, 105, 108
decision making
data-driven, 120, 123
including staff in, 84
responsible, 12–13
DeCosta, D. B., 2, 3
on advocacy, 102–103, 109–110
on cultural responsiveness, 128–129
on culture of care, 36
on daily practices, 26
on expectations, 116–117
on mood sharing, 14
on racial reflection, 68–69, 78
on relationship building, 83–85, 91–93
on school culture, 133–134
on self-care, 53–55, 62–63
on social-emotional learning, 9–10, 32–33
deficit mindsets, 105, 106–107, 146
dehydration, 61
delegation, 60
trust, relationships, and, 85–86
Delpit, L., 38–39
DeMatthews, D., 60, 61, 105
Demo, D. H., 39
demographics, 71
diet, 61, 63
discipline
culture of care and, 37–39
enacting positive practices of, 120, 122

racial bias and, 17
dispositional leadership, 58
distributive leadership, 94–95, 138
divisive political climate, 2
cultural responsiveness and, 37, 117–118
teaching about racism and, 17–18
Drago-Severson, E., 84, 91–92
Dudley, M., 59–60

E

Educational Administration Quarterly, 10
Elias, M. J., 35
Ellison, C. M., 35–36
emotional health, 60
emotional intelligence (EI), 12
definition of, 12, 35
history of, 34
RULER approach and, 24–25
for teachers, 13–14
emotional labor, 58
emotions
behavior problems and, 13
calming, 16, 17
expressing, 16
how much to display, 58
recognizing and dealing with your own, 9–10
RULER approach with, 24–25
self-awareness of, 54, 57–59
sharing, 14
empathy, 10
perspective taking and, 88, 89
empathy interviews, 107–108, 109–110
empowerment
agency and, 95
invisibility syndrome and, 19
racial reflection and, 72
equity
co-creation and co-liberation of, 93–96
racial reflection and, 73–74
schoolwide vision for, 75–77, 127
equity audits, 107–110, 126–127
Esimai, C., 75
ethno-humanist and bureaucrat model of leading, 10
exercise, 61
expectations
before *Brown v. Board*, 119, 126
clear and tangible, 136–137
data-driven decision making and, 120, 123
deficit images and, 105, 106–107
discipline and, 38–39
equity audits and, 109
importance of high, 118–119
nurturing through, 45, 46–47, 115–131, 146
potential action steps on, 131
for professional development, 120, 124–125
questions for reflection on, 129
racial biases and, 71–72
rigorous academics and, 120, 124
safe and nurturing environments and, 120–125
school culture and, 137
student voice and, 120, 121–122
transformational leaders and, 20
transformational leadership and, 21–22
Words From a Principal on, 116–117
Words From a Professor on, 117–118

F

families
advocating for, 101, 104–106
agency of, 95–96
connecting with, 89–91
in creating expectations, 120

cultural responsiveness and, 126, 127
empowerment of, 84
identity statements and, 78
perspective taking and, 89
in racial equity statements, 77
racial reflection and, 73–75, 79
relational trust with, 87–88
family agency, 95–96
feedback, 91–92
in creating safe environments, 121
from families, 96
school culture and, 137, 138
from staff, 88
from students, 95–96
First Amendment rights, 117–118
"5 Elements of a Positive Classroom Environment for Students Living with Adversity" (Zacarian, Alvarez-Ortiz, & Haynes), 107
Five Practices for Equity-Focused School Leadership (Radd, Generett, Gooden, & Theoharis), 73
Floyd, G., 102–103
"4 Practices Serve as Pillars for Adult Learning: Learning-Oriented Leadership Offers a Promising Way to Support Growth" (Drago-Severson), 92
Franklin, A. J., 18
Freire, P., 18, 75
Fuller, K., 119
Furman, G., 21

G
Garner, P. W., 39
Gay, G., 19, 35, 74, 118, 136
Generett, G. G., 73
Glynn, T., 19–20
Goldring, R., 59
Goleman, D., 12, 34
Gomada, 93
Gooden, M. A., 2, 3, 19, 31, 38, 55, 67–68, 71, 72–73, 104, 105, 108
about, 4
on advocacy, 103–104
on CRASEL, 33–34
on empathy and leadership, 10
on racial reflection, 69–70
on relationships, 85–86
on school culture, 135–136
on self-care, 55–57
on students' rights, 117–118
Govan, I. M., 71
Grant, T., 10
growth mindset, 109

H
hair discrimination, 117–118
Halx, M., 95
Hammond, Z., 76, 136
Hanrahan, A. R., 13
Harlem Grown, 62–63
Harrison, L., 37
Haskins, N. H., 74
Hay, C., 76
Haynes, J., 107
healing circles, 122
Helping Teachers Learn: Principal Leadership for Adult Growth and Development (Drago-Severson), 91
Henry, L. M., 139
Higgins, K. M., 38–39
Hilliard, A., 119
hiring practices, 125
historically responsive literacy (HRL) model, 124
Hoffmann, J. D., 12
holistic development, 119
holistic responses, 36–37

Hollins, C. D., 71
honesty, 87
Horne, D. M., 59–60
Howard, T. C., 74–75
HRDQ, 93
HRL model.
  See historically responsive literacy (HRL) model
Hughes, M., 39
Hurd, E., 37

I
identity
  culture of care and, 20–21, 36, 39–40
  HRL model on, 124
  incorporating in the curriculum, 127
  leadership and, 58
Ieva, K., 94
Individualized Education Plans, 109
individual needs, culture of care and, 36–37
instructional practices, culturally responsive, 24
integrity, 86
interventions, 109
invisibility syndrome, 18–19
isolation
  leadership and, 1, 9–10, 85–86
  racial, 73
Ivcevic, Z., 12

K
Keith, V. M., 39
Kelly, S., 18
Khalifa, M. A., 19, 31, 38, 55, 72–73, 75, 87, 104, 105, 108, 126
Kiecolt, K. J., 39
Kirkland, K., 74
Knight, D., 60, 61
Knight-Manuel, M. G., 40
Kupzyk, K. A., 13
Kwon, K., 13

L
Ladson-Billings, G., 19, 35, 95, 118
Lalor, A. D., 107
LaPoint, V., 35–36
Lasater, K., 59
leadership
  advocacy and, 105–109
  biases and, 71–72
  crisis, 59
  critical self-awareness and, 72–73
  culturally responsive school, 19–25
  culture of care and, 37
  distributive, 94–95, 138
  empathy and, 10
  engaging in culturally responsive sustaining, 45, 47
  equity teams, 56
  great man theory of, 85
  growth in, 135–136
  isolation and, 1, 9–10, 85–86
  motivation for, 1
  racial autobiographies and, 67–74
  relationship building and, 83–86
  self-care strategies and, 42, 44–45, 55–56
  self-management and, 57–59
  servant, 89–90
  social justice, 104–105
  student, 116–117, 128–129
  student self-awareness, 23, 134
  teacher agency and, 94–95
  themes of perspectives/practices in, 41–42
  transformational, 20–22, 37, 40–41
Lee, A. T., 74

Leung-Gagné, M., 37
life circumstances, 13, 32–33
    approaches to culture and, 40–41
listening, active, 89
Little, S., 122
Lomotey, K., 20–21, 119
"Looking at Data Through an Equity Lens" (Bocala & Bouidett), 107
Losen, D. J., 37
Lowery, K., 119

M

MacDonald, E., 92
Macfarlane, A., 19–20
Macfarlane, S., 19–20
Maggin, D. M., 38
Mahatmya, D., 39
Malo-Juvera, V., 110
Mansfield, K. C., 95
Marciano, J. E., 40
Marshall, S. L., 75
Marshall, T., 4
Martin, L., 16
Matias, C. E., 17
Maunder, R. E., 122
Mawhinney, H., 105
Mayer, J. D., 12, 24–25, 33–34, 35
Mayer-Salovey-Caruso Emotional Intelligence Test, 33–34
McClain-Meeder, K., 59–60
McCombs, J., 37
"Meeting Student Trauma with an Asset-Based Approach" (Alvarez-Ortiz, Haynes, & Zacarian), 107
mentors, 60
Mercer, K. A., 59–60
Meta-Moment, 24
Meta-Moments, 122
Meyers, C. V., 55
microaggressions, 18, 72
Mid-Atlantic Equity Consortium, 109
Milner, H. R., 38–39
mindfulness, 4, 40
    daily practices of, 22–26
    expectations and, 116
    self-care and, 53–55
    at TMALS, 62–63
misinformation, 2
modeling, 13
    cultural responsiveness, 125, 127
    high expectations, 119, 120–121
    relationships and, 86–87
    self-awareness and, 57–59
    transformational leadership and, 21–22
Mood Meter, 14, 24–25, 62
Moorosi, P., 119
Moreno, A. J., 15–16
motivation, 58, 72
Mould, S., 84
Moule, J., 38–39
Muhammad, G., 41, 119, 124

N

Nagasawa, M. K., 15–16
National Association of Elementary School Principals, 108
National Center for Education Statistics (NCES), 59
Nelsestuen, K., 110
networks and networking, 60, 108–109
"New School Equity Audit Tool" (NAESP), 108
New York State Education Department, 35
norms, 76, 120
Nöthling, J., 16

"Nurturing Through High Expectations Reflection" reproducible, 125, 130

O

O'Doherty, A., 34, 72, 73
oppression
    HRL model and, 124
    internalization of, 18
    self-awareness around, 104–105
    student/family agency and, 95
    suboppression, 18–19
    understanding systems of, 34, 75, 103–104
O'Rear, I., 59
ownership, 96, 122

P

parent associations, 96
partnerships, 45, 47, 133–134, 139–143
    potential action steps for, 143
    questions for reflection on, 141
    Words From a Principal on, 133–134
Pedagogy of the Oppressed (Freire), 18
peer mediation, 122
performance measures, 21
personal regard for others, 86
perspective taking, 88, 89, 127
physical health, 60, 61, 63
Pijanowski, J. C., 59
policies and practices
    alignment of, 137–138
    celebrating best, 140
    challenging exclusionary, 105, 107–108
    culturally responsive, 117–118, 125–129
    reflecting on, 101
    school culture and, 136–138
post-traumatic stress disorder (PTSD), 15–16
"Potential Action Steps" reproducible, 6, 28–29, 50–51, 65, 81, 99, 113, 143
Powell, R., 110
professional development
    approaches to discipline and, 37–38
    collaborative, 76
    culture of care and, 36
    expectations for, 120, 124–125
    teacher agency and, 94–95
professional health, 60
psychological health, 60
Pure Edge, 23, 62, 128

R

race and ethnicity
    approaches to culture and, 40–41
    building common understandings of, 75
    co-creation/co-liberation of equity and, 93–96
    colorblind approach to, 40–41
    critical consciousness and, 34
    curriculum and, 56
    definitions of, 71
    discipline and, 37–38
    invisibility syndrome and, 18–19
    laws against teaching on, 37
    political divisiveness and, 17–18
Race-ing Moral Formation (Walker & Snarey), 43
racial autobiographies, 67–74, 78
"Racial Autobiography Reflection," 80
racial reflection, 67–81
    importance of, 74–75
    potential action steps for, 81
    questions for, 79
    racial autobiographies and, 67–74
    Words From a Principal on, 68–69, 78
    Words From a Professor on, 69–70
racism

advocacy and, 102–113
antiracist stance toward, 20
awareness of the history of, 117–118
conversations about, 16–18
laws against teaching on, 37
systemic, 16–17
Radd, S. I., 73
Randolph, A. W., 119
Ray, J., 59
Ready for Rigor, 136
reflection, 5–6
capacity building for, 72–73
conversations about racism and, 16–18
on CRASEL, 49
on deficit mindsets, 106–107
equity audits and, 107–108
on policies and practices, 101
questions for discussion and, 27
racial, 67–81
racial equity vision and, 75–77
on relationships, 97, 98
self-, 2
on self-care, 63
self-care and, 61, 64
Reilly, E., 119
relational health, 60
relational trust, 86–87
relationships, 83–99, 146
academic achievement and, 11–12
co-creation and co-liberation and, 93–96
CRASEL framework on, 45, 46
culture of care reflected in, 22
importance of trust in, 86–87
leadership and, 58
nurturing through high expectations and, 115–131
potential action steps for, 99
reflection questions on, 97, 98
school culture and, 135
social capital and, 108–109
strengthening community, 87–91
Words From a Principal on, 83–85, 91–93
Words From a Professor on, 85–86
relationship skills, 12–13
reproducibles
"Advocacy Leadership Reflection," 109, 112
"Community Relationship-Building Reflection," 91, 98
"CRASEL Leadership Reflection," 141, 142
"Nurturing Through High Expectations Reflection," 125, 130
"Potential Action Steps," 6, 28–29, 50–51, 65, 81, 99, 113, 143
"Racial Autobiography Reflection," 80
"Self-Care Reflection," 61, 64
respect, 86
restorative circles, 122
Reyes, P., 60, 61
Richards, C., 4, 32, 53
rituals, culturally responsive, 23–24
Rivera-McCutchen, R. L., 20
Rivers, S. E., 12
Roach, S., 69
Robinson, D. V., 119
routines
of care for students, 43
culturally responsive, 23–24
RULER approach, 24–25, 62, 116, 121–122
student leadership and, 128

S

safety, environments of, 15–16, 19

creating, 120–125
discipline practices and, 120, 122
relational trust and, 86–87
social capital and, 108–109
trauma and, 15–16
Salovey, P., 12, 24–25, 33–34, 35
Schneider, B., 86
Schwartz, T., 15–16
Scott, C., 37
Seashore Louis, K., 87
Seedat, S., 16
SEL.
See social-emotional learning (SEL)
self-awareness, 4, 12–13, 57–59, 146
advocacy and, 104–105
critical, leadership and, 72–73
cultural responsiveness and, 74–75
mindfulness and, 53–55
conversations about racism and, 16–18
student leaders for, 23
racial reflection and, 67–81
student leadership and, 116–117
self-care, 42, 44–45, 46, 53–65
areas of, 59–60
definition of, 59
establishing a practice in, 60–63
goals of, 59
importance of, 59–60
potential action steps for, 65
self-awareness and, 57–59
self-management and, 57–59
student leadership and, 116–117
Words From a Principal on, 53–55, 62–63
Words From a Professor on, 55–57
"Self-Care Reflection" reproducible, 61, 64
self-compassion, 10
self-concept, 39–40
self-management, 12–13, 53, 57–59
self-regulation
for leaders, 57–59
trauma and, 15–16
self-sacrifice, 59
Seow, K., 84
serenity spaces, 122
servant leaders, 89–90
service projects, 96
Simmons, D., 16, 17, 18–19, 40
Singleton, G. E., 76
situational leadership, 58
Smith, J., 110
Snarey, J. R., 43, 118
SOAR analysis, 110
social awareness, 12–13
social capital, 105, 108–109
social-emotional learning (SEL), 1, 11–15, 145–146
barriers to, 40–41
benefits and limitations of, 15–19
bridging with CRASEL, 31–51
CASEL framework and, 12–13
cultural responsiveness and, 22–25
daily practices and, 26
definition of, 11, 35
for educators, 13–14
key terms in, 34–36
limitations of, 14
origins of, 11–12
principals and, 9–10
RULER approach in, 24–25
Words From a Principal on, 14
social justice, 2, 4, 19, 40–41, 103–104, 145
centering, 21
leadership and, 41, 97, 104–105

spiritual health, 60
stakeholders, 76, 90, 96
stress
    burnout and, 40, 59
    principals and, 59
    self-care and, 59–60
    trauma and, 15–16
students
    advocating for, 106
    agency of, 95–96
    caring for, 42, 43
    communication with, 88
    in creating expectations, 122
    in creating safe environments, 121
    in data analysis, 120, 123
    deficit images of, 105, 106–107
    leadership by, 116–117, 128–129, 134
    social capital of, 105, 108–109
student voice, 95
    engaging, 120, 121–122
    invisibility syndrome and, 18–19
suboppression, 18
Suliman, S., 16
suspensions, 37–38

T

Taie, S., 59
teacher preparedness programs, systemic racism and, 17
teachers
    advocating for, 106
    agency for, 94–95
    caring for, 43
    in data analysis, 120, 123
    impact of, 56
    intervisitation by, 125
    reflective capacity in, 72–73
    SEL for, 13–14
    social justice leadership and, 104–105
    stress and burnout in, 40
    White privilege and, 72
technology overload, 15–16
Theoharis, G., 73
Thomas, T., 69
"3 Steps to Developing an Asset-Based Approach to Teaching" (Lalor), 107
Thurgood Marshall Academy Lower School (TMALS), 2, 3–4
    bridging SEL and CRSE at, 41
    daily practices at, 26
    equity audit at, 109–110
    leadership opportunities at, 128–129
    professional development at, 76
    racial equity vision at, 76–77
    racial reflection at, 78
    self-care at, 62–63
    trust and relationships at, 91–93
Tillman, L. C., 119
time off, 61
TMALS.
    See Thurgood Marshall Academy Lower School (TMALS)
transparency, 78, 90, 138–139
trauma, 122
trust building and, 15–16
trust, 146
    activities for building, 92–93
    delegation and, 85–86
    importance of, 86–87
    racial reflection and, 72–73
    relationships and, 84–87
    social capital and, 108–109

    social justice leadership and, 104–105
    trauma, SEL, and, 15–16
Tschannen-Moran, M., 139

U

Unearthing Joy (Muhammad), 41, 127
urgency, 105
U.S. Department of Education Office for Civil Rights, 37

V

Vesely, C. K., 39
violence, 15–16
    crisis leadership and, 59
    race-related, 69, 102–103
vision, 2
    collaboration in achieving, 56
    for racial equity, 75–77, 127
    school culture and, 134
    statements of, 77
vulnerability, 10
    leadership and, 78, 138–139

W

Walker, V. S., 43, 118, 119
Weaver, T., Jr., 17
Weiler, J. R., 20–21
well-being
    identity and, 39–40
    self-care and, 59
    trauma and, 15–16
Welsh, R. O., 55
Welton. A., 95
"When Nice Won't Suffice: Honest Discourse Is Kay to Shifting School Culture" (MacDonald), 92
White privilege, 72
whole child education, 35–36
Winton, S., 38
Words From a Principal, 2, 4
    on advocacy, 102–103, 109–110
    on cultural responsiveness, 128–129
    on daily practices, 26
    on expectations, 116–117
    on mood sharing, 14
    on racial reflection, 68–69, 78
    on relationship building, 83–85, 91–93
    on school culture, 133–134
    on self-care, 53–55, 62–63
    on social-emotional learning, 9–10, 32–33
Words From a Professor, 2
    on advocacy, 103–104
    on CRASEL, 33–34
    on empathy and leadership, 10
    on racial reflection, 69–70
    on relationships, 85–86
    on school culture, 135–136
    on self-care, 55–57
    on students' rights, 117–118

Y

Yale Center for Emotional Intelligence, 24–25
Young, J. L., 17
Young, J. R., 17

Z

Zacarian, D., 107
Zalaquett, C. P., 139
Zembylas, M., 17
zero-tolerance policies, 38
Zins, J. E., 35
Zion School, 119

The Antiracist School Leader
Daman Harris

Learn how to plan, test, and execute a comprehensive antiracist vision to transform the culture, curriculum, and conscience of your district and school administration. This book will challenge and empower you to partner with school staff and the community to tackle issues of systemic oppression that have impacted teaching and learning.
BKG081

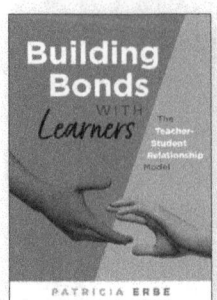

Building Bonds With Learners
Kim Wallace

"The proven process in this book," says author Kim Wallace, "helps leaders keep their equity lens wide open and zeroed in on serving groups of students that have been denied access to a quality K–12 education by responsibly and responsively infusing new initiatives into their organizations."
BKG120

A Blueprint for Belonging
Morgane Michael

Equip educators with a toolbox of clear, concise, and practical strategies to foster a school culture of belonging and positivity. Author Morgane Michael empowers leaders and classroom teachers to construct a school environment that is welcoming and inclusive, providing a strong foundation for student social-emotional and academic success.
BKG185

Be the Driving Force
Don Parker

"*Be the Driving Force* is a powerful resource because it is personal, reliable, and practical," writes educator and author William D. Parker. Principals will discover insightful guidance on building self-confidence, leading with integrity, and ensuring equity in education and culturally responsive practices.
BKG090

Solution Tree | Press

Visit SolutionTree.com or call 800.733.6786 to order.

Global PD teams
Collaborative Learning for School Improvement

Quality team learning **from authors you trust**

Global PD Teams is the first-ever **online professional development resource designed to support your entire faculty on your learning journey.** This convenient tool offers daily access to videos, mini-courses, eBooks, articles, and more packed with insights and research-backed strategies you can use immediately.

GET STARTED
SolutionTree.com/**GlobalPDTeams**
800.733.6786

Solution Tree